MANIPULATION
201

Self-Preservation For a Dark Triad World

R.P. MENTOR TOKYO

Copyright © 2023 R.P. Mentor Tokyo.

All rights reserved. No part of this book may be reproduced, stored, or transmitted by any means—whether auditory, graphic, mechanical, or electronic—without written permission of both publisher and author, except in the case of brief excerpts used in critical articles and reviews. Unauthorized reproduction of any part of this work is illegal and is punishable by law.

Contents

Introduction vi

The Hypothetical 1
Keep Your Head Up 4
See No Evil, Hear ~~No~~ Evil 6
I Can Hardly Contain Myself 10
The Golden Rule 14
Emotional Runoff 16
I Had It, You Got It 18
Tell Me What I Did Wrong 21
It's Been a While, Hasn't It? 24
Throw Him to the Wolves............................. 26
The Appraisal Shop 28
I'd Like a Second Opinion............................ 30
(Im)Plausible Deniability............................. 32
Appeal to Emotion 41
"You Can't Generalize" 44
The Truth in Anger 46
Monkey in the Middle.................................. 48

The "You Must Be Gay" Argument 51
Beware the Siren's Song 53
Induced Conversation 57
Either You Dominate Me, Or I Dominate You ... 59
The Trojan Horse 64
The Power Struggle 67
Indirect Questions 73
Do You Think They Noticed? 76
Precarious Masculinity 78
Living Rent Free in Your Head 79
You Got Me Pregnant! 81
The Tradwife Con 84
Putting Her Best Food Forward 86
I Just Need to Try Harder 89
DESTROY ME! 90
Not All Women Are Like That 93
Complain to Maintain 95
Condition+Phobic=SHAME ON YOU! 97
Clingers 99
Misery Loves Company 104
Arguing For Sport 107
Silence is ~~Golden~~ Manipulation 110
Let's Get to Know ~~Each Other~~ You 111
Guerrilla Validation 113
DON'T TAKE THE BAIT! 115
Pseudo-Projection 117
Man: The Untapped Resource 120

Handling Argumentative People 123
The Marketplace IS NOT Your Pet Shop 126
Could You Do Me a Favor? 134
The Parrot Test 139
The Machiavellian in Me 142
Babe, Meet My Best Friend, Chad! 144
Female-Induced Male Paralysis 147
I'm Done with the Games 149
/noclip 151
Medical Gynocentrism 154
The Bait and Switch 157
Something for Nothing 161
The Fun Police of Stockholm 165
Soul Gazer 169
The Substance of Life 171
I Need to Get Back at Them 173
So, What Can You Do? 175

References 178

Introduction

Welcome, and thank you; by investing in me, you are investing in yourself as the lessons provided herein, I have no doubt *have*, and *will*, affect you—it is just a matter of *when*. I will note, however, to keep this book and what you learn from it a secret except when you really trust someone but perhaps not even then as, to expose this information, can make you a target (see I'm Done with the Games). Why would this be the case? Let this be your first lesson right here in the introduction: by (in)directly exposing what manipulation tactics have worked on you in the past or even that you're educating yourself on this subject, whether perceived of as a challenge and/or weakness, will not have the desired effect of deterring manipulators, but pulling them in.

Manipulators view the world as a *Power Struggle: in their mind, if you're bringing it up or educating yourself on it, it must have worked on you before, so they will likely use it. This especially being the case if they're grandiose, as they may rationalize that they can do a better job than the last person. Manipulators want *something* from you whether it be money, validation, or perhaps you even made them feel insecure about themselves unintentionally, so they're biding their time to get back at you in a sadistic manner when the time is right. Everything is fair game, and this includes your conscientiousness, any emotionality, and even perception that you're a good person resulting in you predictably doing the right thing, which can put you *right* where the manipulator wants you.

It's like the saying goes, "all's fair in love and war," and whether you believe it or not, you *are* in a war. Fortunately for you, however, once you internalize the manipulation tactics detailed in this book, you'll notice that manipulators tend to repeat themselves with little nuance, so you're doing yourself a huge favor by keeping this book close to you as a reference. Let it serve you as a guide to, and

---

An asterisk (*) precedes the capitalized name of an entry on another page in this book.

perhaps, best friend in traversing this Dark Triad (narcissism, Machiavellianism, psychopathy) world as, and make no mistake about it, you *are* alone in this world, with few exceptions. Even in the case of "friends," most people will not want to see you succeed in this life, or at least, more than themselves and such cases commonly result in the desire for sabotage, so trustworthy people are rather hard to come by. Remember too, that everyone has a price, and unbeknownst to you, they might have just gotten paid. So, keep your enemies close, but this book even closer.

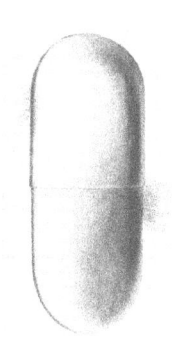

The Hypothetical

Be extremely cautious when people bring up hypothetical scenarios involving you, themselves, or an unknown—perhaps made up—party; perhaps revolving around morally questionable acts. The reason for this is that the manipulator's words may serve as a risk-averse strategy wherein they are directly testing to gain an understanding of how you would react to a similar set of circumstances occurring in real life—something they will attempt in the near future. Example 1: a Japanese woman is testing to see if an American man she is interested in will date her. In attempts at gauging how the man maneuvers relationship dynamics, she forms and presents a hypothetical scenario of a man of a different ethnicity—perhaps presenting this as a scenario her friend is/has gone through. For instance, she may ask, "why would a *Japanese* man continue talking to a woman without bringing up the possibility of dating?" In response, the man states, "well, it may be that the man finds the woman attractive, but simply does not have much interest in dating." Taking this information as indicative of how the man is maneuvering the current situation with her, she proceeds to ghost him. Not a perfect strategy of course, and in this case, the woman may have saved herself some time by implementing it. Example 2: two men are discussing ideas, and one begins to focus on how he has observed that other people commonly steal ideas. The other man agrees, although not displaying strong signs of disapproval—likely due to it not currently happening to him. About a week goes by and the man who initially brought up stealing engages in stealing ideas from the man he asked the question to. In this case, essentially, the bringing up of the subject of stealing was an indirect test to see how the other man would respond to being taken advantage of in this manner. Example 3: a man who has expressed interest in making a business with you but has not displayed a willingness to put in the work meets with you and presents a story about some hypothetical man he had interacted with who has been stealing money from people. A couple of days after this, he insists on you both going into business with a third party you've never met—supposedly a friend of his. Interestingly, this involves signing a non-disclosure agreement and investing funds up front. This is yet another case wherein the hypothetical situation serves to provide the manipulator with a sense of what you would do if they attempted to exploit you. In the case of Example 3, if they *are* able to get you to sign a non-disclosure agreement, this seals the deal as you would not be able to talk about the situation. By being vigilant about presented hypothetical situations, and yes, even that of "friends" (see Appeal to Emotion), they may serve as foreshadowing as opposed to a disconnected conversation followed by seemingly random exploitative acts.

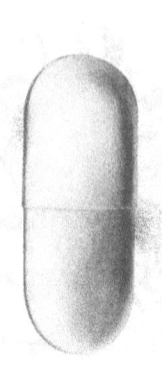

Keep Your Head Up

There are a number of manipulation tactics that are only effective when you don't have access or pay attention to the manipulator's facial expression. Keeping your head up to gauge facial expressions during interactions can prove very helpful in understanding people's intentions regardless of their words. Here is an example of how this may play out as I observed in the workplace: a woman in the office made a simple joke about one of our coworkers. This was not meant to offend, but as I began to laugh a bit, it became rather apparent that this was taken offensively as I watched her facial expression abruptly shift to that of embarrassment as well as aggressive anger. To get back at the coworker that told the joke, she engaged in shifting the woman's attention to a flaw in an item she bought to elicit a negative emotional response and insisted on hyper focusing on it in a sadistic manner which became apparent by the rather large smirk on her face. This was something the coworker that made the joke did not see as she was too focused on the item's flaw. Acts such as this I've observed on multiple occasions wherein either the person is made to focus on something other than the manipulator, or as the situation elicits a negative emotional response in the target, they instinctively tend to look down or away in discomfort. This brings about an air of plausible deniability as the target is never made aware of the intent of the manipulator expressed through facial expressions, and therefore, in subsequent conversations on the event, alternative explanations can be presented which are just plausible enough to keep the target from gaining an objective understanding of what actually occurred. In the context of the provided example, the manipulator could assert that she was bringing the target's attention to the flaw in the item since she thought she would want to know as opposed to the actual reason: a sadistic sense of satisfaction in eliciting a negative emotional response in her. Now, of course, familiarizing oneself with this manipulation tactic is all fine and good; however, if you're someone on the spectrum of autism as I am, I do realize that this may be easier said than done given the tendency to not look people in the eyes, and so I will provide an alternative strategy in the next section.

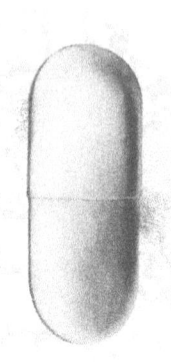

See No Evil, Hear ~~No~~ Evil

Yes, I'm on the autism spectrum, so when speaking with people, I tend to not look them in the eyes. People also tend to do this when they are thinking through what they're saying, so this strategy, I think will prove beneficial for many people as there are many chances for you to miss other people's facial expressions indicative of their intentions as well as manipulative tendencies. Manipulators can be very skilled at what they do; they've likely lived a significant portion of their lives honing these skills, and perhaps even throughout childhood due to familial dynamics and/or even genetics in the case of conditions such as psychopathy. If you are someone who doesn't look people in the eyes, depending on what country you live in, this *can* stick out to manipulators not only as being indicative of dishonesty, but also as a weakness—likely as being a sign of submissiveness and thus making you a target—but

MANIPULATION 201

you can actually use this to your advantage. How? Well, by not looking them in the eyes, the manipulative party—many of them being highly narcissistic—is likely to get cocky, resulting in a sense of comfort, and therefore letting their guard down a bit. When this occurs, as I've observed, they feel more comfortable letting their mask slip which can manifest in overt facial expressions such as smirking and even almost laughing (see also I Can Hardly Contain Myself). Now although you may not be able to see this shift, it is possible to hear it: as research has provided evidence for, emotions are expressed through the body, and to your benefit, including the voice. For instance, a smile tends to—although not invariably—be associated with an increase in vocal pitch; however, smiling has also been accurately recognized in whispers, so go with your gut instinct in determining if a shift in someone's voice is indicative of a smile when not looking them in the face. As manipulation as well as picking up on cues of emotionality in general is nothing new, we surely evolved to pick up on subtle signs that are not always readily available to the conscious mind—hence the ability for people to pick up on a smile in a whisper. Understandably, if you're someone who tends to second guess themselves in judging the emotions of others, you may actually be more accurate in your judgements than you think. Some other good points to keep in mind are as follows:

1. Uncertainty has been associated with a weak voice and an intonation that rises (see also Soul Gazer) meaning the pitch becomes higher towards the end of a word/statement.
2. Deception has been associated with slower speech sometimes as well as an increase in vocal pitch.
3. Honesty has been associated with a falling intonation as well as the voice being louder from the beginning.
4. Unreliable speech in general has been associated with more shifts in talking speed as well as pitch.

There are manipulators—for instance those higher in Machiavellianism as this is associated with leveraging false agreeableness, but realistically the Dark Triad in general—who are well aware of how to mimic honest and even caring speech patterns as a means to behave in a dishonest and/or even sadistic manner. I recall an interesting instance of this while speaking with two married women when I visited America after almost a decade: one explained that she enjoys testing to see the full range of emotional responses she can get out of someone, and surely this includes her husband. I responded, "so you're sadistic," and the other one laughed while responding "yes," followed by emphasizing in a positive manner that her friend will say, according to her, "*the most messed up things*, but make it sound nice." Men's dominant response to certain behavior was also brought up and so I asked the sadistic woman if she liked getting put in her place. This brought about a bit of a strange look on her face and was not answered.

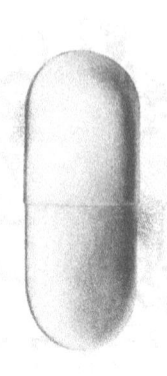

I Can Hardly Contain Myself

Not all manipulators are created equal. Some are highly skilled, but psychopaths tend to be an impulsive bunch, so they can be the ones who can hardly contain themselves due to their ongoing pursuit of instant gratification. While some manipulators maintain a complete poker face throughout their manipulative acts, some display obvious facial cues despite preemptively attempting to conceal them. Various terms pop up in research explaining these displays of affect (emotion) such as duping delight, which is a positive state elicited in anticipation of, during, or after a lie. You can imagine a situation wherein you think you lost something, but actually your coworker hid it. Looking around the office and still not being able to find it, you ask your coworker which elicits a brief smirk, but they claim that they have not seen the item. Cheater's high is similar to duping delight, but the focus is

MANIPULATION 201

on a positive state being elicited by having behaved unethically. Look out for aggressive eyes as well as the perching of one's lips which creates a bit of a rounded O formation as they are purposely forcing the lips together as if to hold a straw in place. This can be referred to as a suppressed smile in literature and is a preemptive measure to prevent a full-on smirk, but a failing one in that it doesn't fully stop the edges of the mouth from spreading outward, and in the same manner that you may have observed someone attempt to hold in laughter, the face tends to twitch. It is to your benefit that social interactions are fast paced enough that manipulators can't hide their true intentions/feelings sometimes. For example, smirking may be expressed when they say something wherein a smirk is not the response you would expect and can be indicative of their words as well as actions serving to manipulate you in some way. They may also preemptively feed you pleasant-sounding traits they supposedly harbor, but this is just to get your guard down such as emphasizing their religiosity which is nonexistent or stating that they are an honest person (see I'm Done with the Games). Conversely, they may resort to expressing unpleasant realities about themselves as a last resort. It is interesting that direct, as opposed to covert language, and furthermore, honesty, can be a last resort for many women, but also people higher in the Dark Triad in general. This is where you end up with the woman who wore a mask of faithfulness throughout the relationship, gets caught, and then opens up about her past; perhaps even familial dynamics they were aware all along may have contributed to their behavior which is an extreme measure implemented in the hopes of eliciting a compassionate response. They may plead how they are the way they are because they had, for instance, a horrible mother, and this may very well be true, but you must also keep in mind that it took them behaving in a manipulative, as well as, perhaps, sadistic manner up to the perceived end of the relationship for them to acknowledge this as well as claim that they will change, which tells you everything you need to know. This is rather telling as it lets you know they were aware of all of their dysfunctional behaviors all along. If the manipulator is sadistic, this may come down to the hope they can pull you back in despite their past behavior for further abuse (see Clingers for more on this). Additionally, like a ghost with unfinished business, but also an apt analogy as your responses are in large part modified by the woman's outer neotenous figure (see Putting Her Best Foot Forward) while the inside is hollow—a ghost in the shell, if you will—this may serve to provide them further access to you, meaning more chances to acquire whatever desired resource they had in mind, and likely from the start of the relationship.

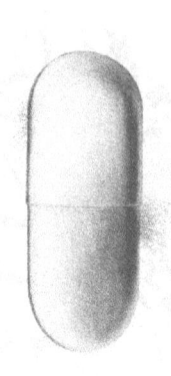

The Golden Rule

Of the people I've had to discard in my life, they all had one thing in common: an elicited look of anger or being upset when honestly providing information. For instance, in the case of one perceived narcissist, I explained my social limitations and that I require alone time which resulted in him looking angry, but as tends to be the case in these situations, he didn't explain why and quickly adjusted his facial expression. In another case while in a group, I explained the negative aspects of gossip which elicited an angry facial expression on a woman (see The Truth in Anger). Smirking at inappropriate times such as when you explain a negative event that has impacted your life is another dead giveaway when it comes to those who likely want to see you fail. Luckily for you, the act of smirking tends to not be held back which I've always found interesting as, in my eyes, it means they're not aware they're doing it, just don't care, or perhaps even gain sadistic supply through observing the response they get to such a facial expression. Manipulators have self-serving plans for you which likely go against what you know to be in your best interest, so be careful and remain observant when interacting with anyone and everyone. As the expression of anger is indicative of the manipulator's realization that something is going against what they find to be in their best interest, in the event it is you who elicits this response, and especially when you are stating what is reasonably in *your* best interest, do realize that they may have exploitation on the mind.

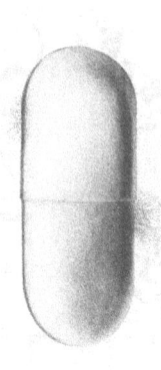

Emotional Runoff

There is a manipulation tactic I term Emotional Runoff which can be implemented, consciously or unconsciously, as follows: in a brief video wherein a woman talks about the problem with men sleeping with other women's wives, she states "let me be very clear, women are not children they're adults, and they're absolutely responsible for their own actions. *But*, there used to be a time where good men looked out for women and protected them because they're more vulnerable. When good men didn't take up every woman simply because she had herself on offer. When good men did not walk through every single open door just because it was open and a little bit alluring." In this example, you can imagine the text as a body of water; however, the segment stating that women are "more vulnerable" is a substance infecting the rest of it. As a consequence of this, any other body of water or even person who makes contact with this contaminated water may become infected—of course, depending on a multitude of factors such as one's immune system (knowledge). This is demonstrated in the convenient use of the unrelated notion that women are more "vulnerable" in this context to elicit a more compassionate response in listeners, and this would have the effect of facilitating hypoagency as the emotional response essentially shifts the focus of the listener from women being actors to objects here.

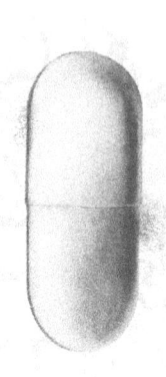

I Had It, You Got It

Manipulators want some form of resource from you, and your time is one of them which they may feel entitled to. This is a highly narcissistic trait and commonly plays out in a similar manner as follows: you elect to provide someone with advice as they had requested it. To you it's no big deal, and you're glad to help them out. We do, however, want to keep in mind that this task does require the investment of resources such as time. So, you discuss the subject they were interested in with them, and they seem pleased. They might even be getting some positive results from your talk. You notice one additional thing, however: their requests to have you provide them with advice are not only progressively *increasing*, but that they want you to help them with things they could obviously do themselves. They're not taking the advice to become independent but are electing to establish a system of dependence. To you,

MANIPULATION 201

it's almost as if they've decided to wash their hands of the many burdens of thought and have decided that this part of their life is taken care of, so now they can focus on other things—in essence, I Had It, You Got It. Noticing this, you decrease the amount of time you're willing to spend aiding the other individual. Instead of the other person being grateful for your help thus far, they attempt to guilt trip as well as shame you. This is an interesting method of attempting to get others to do what you want and only makes sense if it is perceived that the receiver possesses some form of emotional connection wherein they will feel bad about expressing a bit of self-interest. The idea appears to be that they believe they can leverage your emotions in their favor in order to continue receiving some form of resource. Additionally, the need to engage in this behavior is indicative of the person's desperation, and functions much in the same way as an ultimatum: either do what I want, or you're a bad person. The same framework parallels with a woman attempting to bully a man into marriage: either marry me, or I'm leaving, *and* you're a bad person. Be cautious about who you choose to help in life because the other person may have it in their mind that by you agreeing to help them once, this is indicative of an indefinite agreement to keep providing them with resources in the future. I've even seen people try to defend this behavior, and unsurprisingly, these tend to be the same individuals who engage in this behavior. The comments of these individuals can be quite telling regarding their entitlement. Perhaps they'll state something along the lines of a value system based in *Pseudo-Projection: "you should feel good knowing someone trusts you enough to come to you for advice." There are a number of things I believe need to be unpacked when met with such a comment. First and foremost, it's not up to other people to decide for you the feeling elicited from coming to them for advice. This is purely based in self-interest, entitlement, and perhaps narcissism. I stated this to be a pseudo-projected value system in that the individual making such a statement may not even value this supposed state of feeling "good knowing someone trusts you," but is simply presenting this narrative in the hopes it sticks as it possesses the capacity to be perceived of as moral but is ultimately self-serving. Conversely, and although not necessarily a manipulation tactic, you will have people who, when corrected on something, become highly resentful of the source. Where manipulation *can* come into play here is if these individuals become *Clingers.

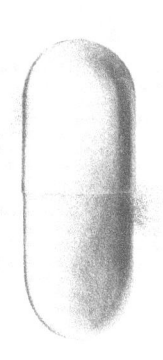

Tell Me What I Did Wrong

This is one tactic many men—especially compassionate ones—fall prey to as they are not prone towards viewing their relationship with their "partner," or women in general, as a *Power Struggle. You don't know what you don't know; and what you do know is informed by a variety of factors including upbringing but also genetics which, in both cases, probably aren't doing you very many favors when considering the sadistic as well as manipulative behavior women so casually engage in today. Commonly, women will insist following their manipulative behavior—perhaps when the man decides to end the relationship—that a conversation take place—that they "talk about it." While the woman may pretend that she has some remorse regarding her behaviors up to that point—notably following behaving in a sadistic manner that she got enjoyment out of—it is part of her game, and what she wants is for you to educate her about any weak points in her manipulation tactics. Perhaps she will say something along the lines of, "I don't know where things went wrong" or "I don't know when you started to hate me so much." She wants *you* to educate her in order to become a better manipulator, as to gain insight into exactly when her manipulation tactics failed her, is to expand her knowledge on what exactly she needs to fix. This being, best case scenario, in the form of a redo with you if you take her back, but if not, for the next relationship. Notably, this is a tactic of choice for women colluding with each other to manipulate a particular man (see Monkey in the Middle). Alternatively, in the context of a workplace, your boss may tell you that they hope you feel comfortable enough to tell them what bothers you which serves the multifaceted purpose of pinpointing how they can elicit a negative emotional response in you in the future (sadism) as well as having you call them out which lets them know what tactics you notice and which you don't. In the case of the former, they may change things up a bit in the future; and as for the latter, they will continue to implement them. One particular instance comes to mind here wherein a narcissistic individual insisted that I express more emotion through speech during my videos. This was accompanied with an angry facial expression

MANIPULATION 201

(see the Truth in Anger), but they quickly became aware of this, and shifted to an attempted smile which looked more like a smirk. As this was someone who would purposely attempt to elicit negative emotional responses, they were surely trying to use my content as a gauge for what to say in the future to satiate their sadistic needs. Think of yourself as a real-time strategy-based video game for women who will perpetually attempt to manipulate, and thus, dominate you.

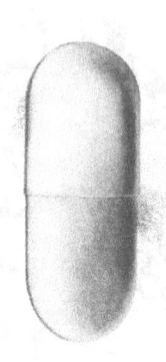

It's Been a While, Hasn't It?

Put simply, those who push for mundane conversation with you out of the blue, may want something from you. Whether the person is even aware of it or not, this dynamic serves to establish rapport—perhaps leveraging that which was established in the past—so as to pave the way for acquiring some form of resource from you in the present. The idea is pretty simple: if someone hasn't spoken to you in years, then suddenly asking for a favor will likely result in failure. If positive conversation is made prior to making the request, however, then there is a higher chance that this will circumvent your sense that they only messaged you for personal gain. The goal is to make it appear as though the delayed request was by chance and not premeditated as opposed *the* purpose of making contact to begin with. In all actuality, if they didn't perceive that they could gain something from you, they likely would never have made contact to begin with. I think most people have experienced this at some point in their lives, and perhaps on some level, have even engaged in it.

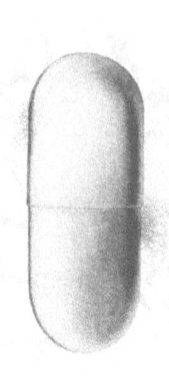

Throw Him to the Wolves

It is true that many men, in the event you display no interest in blindly pursuing women as they are addicted to, will resort to shaming you as a way to get you to conform; but there is another benefit to engaging in this behavior. By getting you to conform (see also Guerrilla Validation), this gives them room to exploit you by Throwing You to the Wolves, meaning to push you to be the one who makes initial contact with women in a bar or club setting. This is beneficial as, whether they're aware of the psychology behind it or not, by having you go first, this not only takes the pressure off them to initiate the first encounter, but also show interest. As Whitchurch and Wilson have explained, when interest is known, people are able to form a story as to why which makes things less interesting. When there is an element of mystery, however, this tends to get stuck in the person's mind as they can't figure things out through the forming of a story. In one interesting study, amongst men who the female participants were informed liked them the most, liked them to an average extent, or that they were uncertain liked them, the women not only found the men in the uncertain group the most attractive, but thought about them the most. In fact, in order of which men were thought of most, it was the uncertain group, followed by the men who liked them to an average extent, and last the men who liked them the most. By throwing you to the wolves which allows them to be fashionably late to the party, there is an advantage as it becomes more of an obligation for them to join in rather than a display of interest. And by joining in while displaying indifference to the women present, this is perceived of as a cue of having abundance (e.g., options, resources). Of course, if the initiator is rather skilled in setting a first impression, such a situation can play to their benefit.

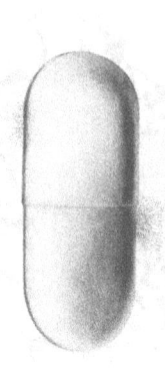

The Appraisal Shop

Back when I used to drink and was still a university student, I recall a time when a male roommate of mine had brought some women over to our apartment. These women were familiar with me as we all attended the same university; however, they knew nothing about me, and so they started asking me questions about myself. At some point in the conversation, they started talking about going out to a club and that I should go with them. This made their faces light up; one of them stating with a rather large smile, "you should come; I've never seen you in a club." *She had never seen me in a club...* what did she mean by this? This assertion appears to come down to the onset of a positive emotional state in anticipation of being able to gauge a man's marketplace value in real time, and in an expedited manner given the dynamics that play out specifically in locations such as clubs as well as bars, or rather,

The Appraisal Shop. In this sense, dopamine, as it is an anticipatory hormone for some form of reward, may be playing a role in the large smile elicited when the women though about me attending a club with them. The key word here being *with*, as there is the additional benefit that if other women find the man in these situations desirable, it increases their status by proxy. This, of course, would only be the case if the man is not found creepy by other women, and if he is not, his presence will be of benefit to her sense of self-worth through increasing her status. In this sense, the women are actively seeking an appraisal for the man as they are prone towards mate copying. In such social settings, a man's suitability as a partner for a hookup or the long-term becomes all the more clear in accordance with how other women respond to him. In essence, if she wants him, I want him too. This especially being the case if women higher in attractiveness and status also display interest. Notably as well, this club would be the first stop as women tend to value other women's opinions more.

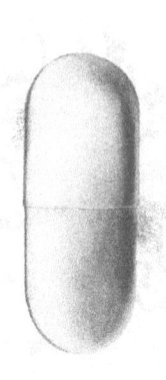

I'd Like a Second Opinion

Marketplace dynamics will be relevant when it comes to interactions between the sexes; and in the same manner that you may Like a Second Opinion when it comes to a doctor's diagnosis, women, may pursue a second appraisal by means such as getting men to additionally attend a gay bar or club with her. Perhaps the first doctor's diagnosis was wrong or misleading, and similarly, perhaps not enough information was obtained from the woman observing the man at a straight bar or club. Essentially, she wants to make sure she's not making a mistake prior to progressing things with the man. Additionally, this may serve as yet another sadistic testing behavior in that it permits her to observe and enjoy the man's discomfort if he is not comfortable in this environment, but the man's agreement to accompany her would furthermore likely be a signal to her that he is, to some extent, invested in her as he is willing to go with her to a location she is aware he has no interest in going to.

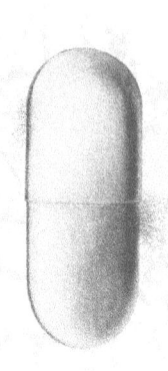

(Im)Plausible Deniability

For many people, at least those who remain skeptical, and as a consequence, seek out answers in this technological age (likely you since you bought this book and good for you by the way), technology is freedom. It is freedom because, understandably, in the past you would more or less only have word of mouth to go off of when attempting to gauge objective reality. It is true that men tend to be higher in trait intellect meaning that, on average, they are more interested in abstract ideas. As a consequence of this, it does appear that they have taken to the internet to gain a better understanding of women's behavior—an endeavor women have historically taken to through word of mouth amongst themselves which has provided them quite the advantage with men being left in the dark. This was made possible not only due to women's ability to read men more effectively than the other way around in most cases—seemingly in a similar way that narcissists read those they perceive as sources of supply—but also that they commonly resort to providing men plausibly deniable answers to their intentions. Men, as they instinctively tend to view women more so on the object side as opposed to agents that act in the world, furthermore contribute to women's ability to get away with this. You may have observed negative behaviors by women such as pairing with "bad boys" which was then written off by men as either the woman being tricked—perhaps in the form of a relationship that lasted multiple years—or simply not knowing what she was doing. This is how men directly facilitate women's hypoagency and women use this to their advantage for purposes such as playing both sides of the short- as well as long-term mating strategy field (i.e., a dual mating strategy). It should come as no surprise by now, but women not only crave a drama-rich environment—notably a characteristic of being higher in the Dark Triad—but dominance (see Either You Dominate Me, Or I Dominate You and The Power Struggle) which elicits sexual arousal. This common assertion by women that they like "nice guys" appears to be an act in plausible deniability through lying by omission that serves the function of facilitating a long-term mating strategy for not only herself, but perhaps other women in accordance with a female in-group bias. I recall an instance wherein, upon a woman stating that the men present just needed to be a "nice guy," my response was to laugh a bit. Her response? A slight smirk, perhaps as if to say, he gets it, or at least a response indicative of her acknowledging that her words were not fully honest. I'm sure you've heard women state something along the lines of "you'll make a great boyfriend to the right woman someday" or "if we're both single at 30, let's get together." These are the same women asserting that men, more specifically the compassionate men more susceptible to their neotenous traits who would pair with them for the long-term, just need to be "nice" and the "right woman" will come along one day. And naturally, these men will ask themselves a four-word question: When is that day? The answer is when the woman is done having hookups and trying to lock down a man higher in the Dark Triad who they have no chance with but provides them the drama-rich environment that they desire. These men are more dominant, manipulative, and furthermore prone towards a short-term mating strategy as well as mate poaching. This is part of why women love bars and clubs so much: they are chaotic locations teeming with men exhibiting Dark Triad traits who are always available for them to scratch that drama-rich

MANIPULATION 201

dominance itch. In the same way that women in academia, as Dr. Cory Clark shed light on, have colluded in order to censor research that, although true, may paint groups in a negative light, so too have they resorted to colluding, censoring, and lying by omission about how their attraction functions in order to keep as many men within their available partnering pool as long-term mates as possible. She also stated that "men are relatively more interested in advancing what is empirically correct and women are relatively more interested in advancing what is morally desirable." Similarly, I would say that while men are more interested in advancing how women's attraction objectively functions, women are more interested in advancing pseudo-altruistic narratives about themselves as a means to simultaneously play on both sides of the mating field. It's sleep with the "bad boy" and cry to the compassionate backup mate to obtain victim status in their eyes. Unsurprisingly, as one study found, when women were exposed to men high in dominance, this made them less satisfied with their current partner, so it shouldn't come as a surprise when women insist on the occasional girl's night out, as the backup mate who serves emotional functions such as the shoulder to cry on— likely an act to draw the man closer to her as he can't stand to see her in supposed pain—although can effectively play the role of provider in the long-term, *cannot* fulfil her sexually. The sweet spot for women is to sadistically trick men into thinking that she desires him in order to extract his resources, so even if there is a "right woman" out there for a particular man, or at least one that wouldn't be of detriment to him, Dark Triad women's pursuit of self-interest through exploiting men ensures that they are less than likely to meet. As was brought up in one study focusing on how psychopaths use humor, "in some of the case observations reported by Cleckley and others, psychopaths react with laughter when being confronted with an obvious lie. One might interpret this in a sense of laughing at those who believed the lie or who have been fooled." This parallels directly with common reports by men wherein, upon confronting a girlfriend or spouse on some manipulative behavior or lie, her response was to smile and giggle. I suspect that this desire to manipulate may even explain some instances of women colluding with men higher in the Dark Triad wherein they avail themselves sexually to them while extracting resources from a more compassionate man. In this sense, these assertions of men needing to be "nice" may come down to malicious manipulative acts by some women coupled with the overt joy expressed in succeeding in this (see I Can Hardly Contain Myself).

MANIPULATION 201

By having the man around and acquiescing to her demands while she is actively manipulating him, he serves as a constant source of sadistic supply/entertainment as well as reminder of her superiority. Paternity fraud, in some cases, may function in the same manner as women commonly select affair partners that are similar to their long-term manipulated partners. We live in a society that directly facilitates women's psychopathy through their infantilization. Men *and* women alike will say men just need to pick the right women, but, again, women themselves would not let them do this if there even was a "right" one to begin with. Once a woman acknowledges that a certain man possesses resources she desires, in a competitive manner so as to beat out her competition, she will mold herself in order to better her chances of obtaining them. Men are starting to realize the truth about this and are exiting the marketplace instead of being exploited as sources/fountains of untapped resources. I'll give you an example I've personally observed of how this plays out in real life, and in a more common manner than any man may want to accept—this especially being the case if it happened to him—and of course, any woman would want men to understand: at an after-wedding party, the many guests were taking pictures of the bride and the groom. The groom goes in for a kiss, and the bride's visceral response to this was a brief look of disgust and to recoil. To add a bit of context to this, the bride, prior to marrying this safe groom, was paired with a typical "bad boy." Shortly after this relationship ended, she was paired with her then groom who does not provide the same stimulation (drama-rich environment; dominance), which likely explains this visceral response—she's just not that into him. This is why sitting back and observing people can be so beneficial in gaining an objective understanding of what's really going on, and the realities people try to hide. As social interactions are so fast paced, even if a person runs scenarios in their head preemptively in order to conceal information, they can always be caught off guard, and this is where you end up with examples such as this one. Even in front of friends and family, the bride could not conceal her underlying psychology: that she is not at all attracted to the man she just married only hours prior. There is also the factor of women's neotenous traits waning over time which results in compassionate men naturally redirecting their attention to younger women in the event women squander their youth trying to lock down a Dark Triad man. Not only this, but women have to deal with another issue taking men's precious resources away from them: the "problem" of sex robots, which has

MANIPULATION 201

been another concern they have voiced their opinions on; again, by using plausible deniability, however, in stating that by men gaining access to these robots, it would lead to violence as well as the objectifying of women. This notion that men are going to "objectify women" due to access to sex robots is a nonsensical argument, and especially when considering that women objectify themselves. It is a dishonest argument perpetuated by women as they view these robots as competition, so they'll use reputation destruction—in this case, on an inanimate object—as they want to be the objects of men's desires in order to continue to garner their resources as well as attention. There is an important question I think it would behoove men to ask themselves: what is the natural response women have to you? For women, their facial structure elicits a compassionate response, but this is not the case for men, and why it makes sense that you do not see women taking care of them in relationships. Men, on the other hand, are more than willing to take care of women in the same manner as they would a household pet as, in both cases, how the pet or woman looks elicits a compassionate response, so they are willing to trade resources for affection. The man may get joy out of observing the woman's smile as he would a dog getting excited to see its bowl being filled. Women seemingly mimic these visceral compassionate responses men express towards them as a consequence of their neotenous traits, which results in the man projecting. This furthermore makes sense of this reverse beauty and the beast dynamic the is quite common today: while the woman mimics the man early on, allowing him to falsely perceive that her psychology functions the way his does, when commitment has been obtained in the form of marriage, she becomes the monster the man is expected to put in her place (see also Beware the Siren's Song). This is in part because she is trying to force the man to fulfil her need for dominance as well as a drama-rich environment that she became used to receiving from hooking up with Dark Triad men, and when things don't work out as the man is lower in the Dark Triad, it is predominantly the woman looking for the door. Yet another pseudo-altruistic narrative women have successfully perpetuated as being due to deadbeat men, but in reality, it is deadbeat women.

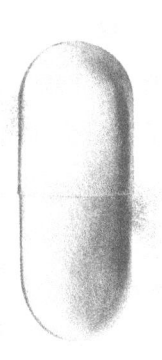

Appeal to Emotion

This can be a bit of a difficult one to deal with as it essentially forces you to adopt the mindset that you really can't trust anyone. Manipulators, once they pinpoint what you're susceptible to—weak points in their eyes—can and will use it against you. Appeal to Emotion is when your perceived weak point is your tendency to be compassionate towards others (see also You Got Me Pregnant!). One way this can play out is as follows: you've been working on a project for some time now and it's starting to get traction. A *Clinger, however, has been noticing this, and as they harbor jealousy and are sadistic, wants to take what you have. Noticing that you are compassionate towards others and even them given that you haven't put your finger on their Clinger tendencies, they start getting you to help them on a similar project which you're more than happy to help with. Things are going fine for a while, but you start to realize that they are engaging in semi-covert self-serving tactics such as stealing ideas and shifting them slightly to make it appear as though they created it. Plausible deniability also plays a role here as, due to the slight shifts, despite the fact that they are essentially regurgitating your ideas, it becomes a bit hard to tell whether this is what they are doing or not. Friendship is also leveraged here in order to lower your guard. In these cases, you'll want to go with your gut instinct, and in the event you cut contact—as this whole ordeal was initiated with the goal of taking from you—they may resort to repeatedly messaging you in desperation to get back on course. These messages will likely be further Appeals to Emotion such as, "did I do something wrong?" (see Tell Me What I Did Wrong), "hey, just checking up on you," and/or, "I thought we were friends." If you respond, their goal will be to pinpoint why this cutting of contact occurred by engaging in further questioning. Upon providing this information, they will then resort to providing plausibly deniable reasons why you are misunderstanding the situation; the exact same tactic women commonly use when they come to realize a man does not get into relationships with women, and furthermore serving the same purpose to desperately get the source of some desired resource back on track for exploitation.

Manipulators will purposely pursue, and furthermore exploit, the title of "friend" as a form of shield as well as way to slip in self-serving manipulative acts such as stealing ideas. They feel entitled to exploit you or that your guard will be down significantly enough when they are considered a friend. Notably as well, threats to getting you back on track such as mutual friends on social networking platforms will be brought up preemptively to plant the seed that they're bad people, but in all actuality, what the manipulator asserts the person did is likely some variant of what they did to them.

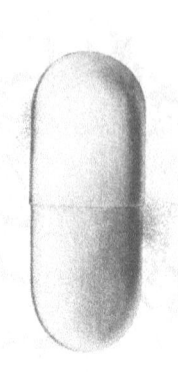

"You Can't Generalize"

In seemingly the majority of cases, women don't rebut, they deflect. If you're reading this, you've surely heard multiple women when confronted with an obvious tendency or behavior she, as well as other women engage in, respond not with a logical statement that would in any way disproving what was said is true, but instead resorts to saying something along the lines of, "well, men do it too." Even going as far back as E. Belfort Bax's 1908 book, *The Fraud of Feminism*, in response to acknowledging women's hysteria, the typical response was that men had it too. Women will exploit the term "generalization" in the same manner as the term "conspiracy theory" is used in place of a legitimate rebuttal to what has been said. The goal of course here being to downplay the legitimacy of a logical argument, and perhaps even accompanied by anger—an elicited emotional response indicative of a perceived threat to something found to be in someone's best interest as explained by authors Jason Weeden and Robert Kurzban (see The Truth in Anger). Interestingly, although perhaps not unsurprisingly, women commonly state that "You Can't Generalize" in response to bringing to their attention a behavior they don't find flattering. In the case of flattering tendencies, however, there is never an argument, and the behavior is simply accepted, but more likely, exaggerated (see also The Marketplace IS NOT Your Pet Shop). Interestingly as well, in the instances I've observed of women reacting negatively due to overhearing a "generalization" regarding women, as soon as it was made clear that it was not about them specifically, they instantly calmed down, accepted what was being stated, and in some cases actually agreed. It appears that this has to do with saving face when perceived to be guilty—rightfully so or otherwise—by association to the word "women." An alternative method I've observed which works well in getting women to accept a reality of typical female behavior is stating that it is an evolved trait. This presumably permits them to feel as though it is natural, and therefore, acceptable, as it implies they have no control over it. In essence, you are leveraging women's proclivity towards hypoagency to obtain an honest response.

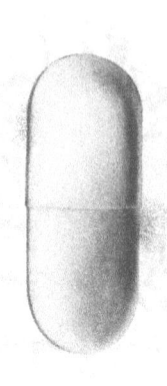

The Truth in Anger

In Jason Weeden's and Robert Kurzban's interesting book, *The Hidden Agenda of the Political Mind*, they shed light on an aspect of the emotion of anger that is rather helpful to understand when it comes to gauging the people around you: from an evolutionary perspective, emotions—although generally thought of as irrational—serve as guides for obtaining self-interested outcomes. For instance, jealousy serves the purpose of eliciting a state of vigilance in relation to a partner's fidelity as a threat has been detected (think mate guarding). Likewise, The Truth in Anger is that it can also be elicited following the detection of a threat to one's self-interest. This can be helpful as the expression of this emotion implies the chance of some form of consequence (e.g., violence) affecting the source of the anger which can deter them from engaging in the causative behavior in the future. For instance, a woman watches an R.P.

Mentor Tokyo video about manipulation and sends angry messages by comment or e-mail. My content is viewed as a threat to the effectiveness of the behaviors she engages in—an important factor likely denied or omitted in the e-mail, however—and so she lashes out. Now, in the case of this woman, she may not rationalize that this is why she feels so compelled to contact me; however, there will be manipulative people who leverage false anger on purpose as they know it can deter people from going against what they find to be in their best interest. When people get angry at hearing the truth, know that this is the reason, and so you're likely on the right track.

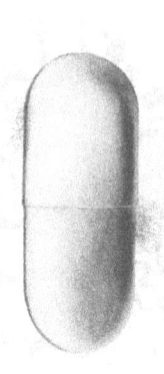

Monkey in the Middle

2022 and 2023 have been two rather insightful years for me as I was exposed to more Dark Triad people targeting me than I can recall throughout my life. Now interestingly, it was rarely just one of them at a time; there would be at least one other party colluding with them in attempts at accomplishing a certain goal. Women crave a drama-rich environment meaning they are higher in the Dark Triad than has been previously thought. Outside of consuming copious amounts of "reality" television, they can resort to realizing such an environment not only with their "partner"—more accurately victim, I would say—in the form of domestic terrorism, but also in the workplace. This comes in the sadistic form of testing (e.g., seeing if the man will call them out on their manipulative behaviors), purposely pursuing negative emotional responses, and view this as a game wherein they may collude with

MANIPULATION 201

other women while gaslighting the man to attempt to make it appear as though they aren't doing anything. Further contributing to the efficacy of this strategy and thus ensuring the game goes on indefinitely, in the event the man picks up on at least one member of the group, feigned innocence and even pseudo-compassionate behavior creating the illusion of being on the man's side is further used in order to garner more information to provide to the group. The tactic of *Tell Me What I Did Wrong is commonly used here as well as playing on the man's masculinity in asserting that the "masculine" thing to do is continue to participate in their game instead of running away (see Precarious Masculinity). This, of course, is not overtly stated as it would expose the existence of the game but insinuating that the man is less masculine for withdrawing his presence from the colluding women can be leveraged, and likely from one pretending to be on the man's side. This is similar to the *You Must Be Gay Argument proposed when a man is not interested in dating a particular woman: it is an exploitation of language meant to elicit certain emotional/behavioral responses. How Monkey in the Middle works is the women—perhaps coworkers or a group of girlfriends/wives—will secretly speak amongst themselves about what they have been getting away with so as to provide education, but it also becomes a running joke, and furthermore, a form of entertainment. Notably, psychopaths tend to prefer humor based around manipulating and outsmarting others. The women will also attempt to one up each other in the process as there exists a competition aspect. Throughout this process the manipulators can push for conversations with the target containing *Indirect Questions meant to check if the manipulation tactics of the group have been working or even noticed. And in the event you cut contact with the manipulators, they may periodically attempt to make contact as if nothing happened—perhaps asking unrelated questions; ones they could get answered by someone else—likely to see if they can somehow pull you back into their game by letting time pass. Needless to say, this whole dynamic is inherently sadistic, and as Dr. Sam Vaknin has proposed, *all* sadists *are* psychopaths. Perhaps it is not for nothing that so many men bring up that they have had at least one psychopathic ex-girlfriend. Such gameplaying *will* run the span of the relationship, whether in a workplace, or "romantic" relationship.

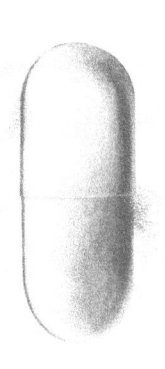

The "You Must Be Gay" Argument

This is a common argument asserted by women and can commonly be accompanied by a smirk which is one sign that the woman is being manipulative. I'll note here that smirking is one sign that manipulators generally don't attempt to conceal—perhaps a sign of impulsivity (see I Can Hardly Contain Myself) to the point that they don't even realize they're doing it—so you can use this to your benefit. As women inherently view men as sources of untapped resources for themselves or other women in accordance with an inherent in-group bias, insinuating that the man may be gay works as men are heavily averse to being perceived of as such. Now why would this be the case? Well, from a reproductive standpoint, this narrative spreading to other women may be perceived of as costing him reproductive opportunities. On some level, I do think that women are well aware of how this argument functions given that they are sadistic, resulting in constantly prodding men for negative emotional responses, and therefore it comes as no surprise that they would leverage the notion of being gay as men so readily express overt anger when associated with the word. At the argument's core, it is rather narcissistic if asserted genuinely, as it implies that women—but more so in particular, the arguer—are so great that there's no way a man could pass such a woman up, and therefore the only possible reason is that he's gay. This is generally not what is at play here, however, and hence the smirk: what the woman is doing is using language as a means to an end in order to elicit a desired emotional response as this state has the perceived potential to produce a desired response. A mix of hurt given that, perhaps, being denied made the woman feel this way and so she lashes out, an unconscious fear of the loss of reproductive opportunities on the part of the man, but ultimately, submission.

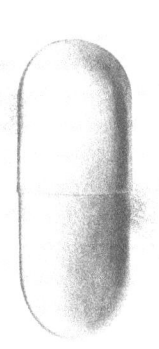

Beware the Siren's Song

Although there are varying interpretations of the nature of these creatures, in accordance with the most commonly used one, this is an apt analogy for how relationships function today and have for some time. Men are instinctively drawn in by traits in women found beautiful; however, as with the depictions of sirens in media, women lure men into a state of vulnerability—commonly in the form of marriage—which leads to an unpleasant death. While a siren may sing or call to a man to pull him overboard a stable ship to drown him, women will *Put Their Best Foot Forward—a mixture of pleasant personality as well as physical traits—which entices the man—sometimes in a manner that could only be explained as a trancelike state—only to pull him from a stable life into one of chaos as she harbors a Dark Triad need for a drama-rich environment. Like the siren as well, women commonly end up killing the man in myriad ways such as their drive, perceptions of reality, mental health, and even that of the physical. At least with the siren, the process is a rather quick one, although traumatic nonetheless; women, on the other hand, will slowly drown the man with her need for chaos over the course of, perhaps, multiple decades throughout a marriage if she doesn't divorce him, he decides to leave, or, he succumbs to the stress of such an arrangement. One such method of killing the man is through criticism: as Dr. Warren Farrell pointed out in his book, *The Myth of Male Power*, one reason men are more likely to develop heart disease may have to do with the research finding that criticism actually elicits an adverse state in the heart wherein an abnormal pulse may develop. As he states specifically regarding the severity of this, "abnormalities as great as those produced by riding a stationary bicycle to the point of either exhaustion or chest pain." Now, this is not at all to say that men should not be exposed to genuine criticism; however, women engage in a malicious form of criticizing as well as disrespecting their "significant others" which is not only sadistic in nature but aims to hurt them. That a gender gap exists when it comes to the rates at which men and women develop heart disease—men being around two times more likely to get it—while there will be multiple reasons for this (e.g., hormones), I find it highly plausible that women play a significant contributory role in all of this. Groups of wives, girlfriends, and even female coworkers will collude with each other in order to satiate their desire for a drama-rich environment wherein the men present (i.e., husbands, boyfriends, male colleagues) become the target for a sort of manipulation Olympics (see Monkey in the Middle for more on this); and unbeknownst to the men, the women are colluding to see what they can get away with at the men's expense as a form of entertainment as well as educating each other on what worked and what didn't. For instance, I've observed a woman engage in rather psychopathic impulsive behaviors, and who would incessantly test men, claim she had ADHD which worked for a while. Another woman she was colluding with was not able to breach a target man's boundaries, but they needed the game to continue, so this other woman began to insist that she also had ADHD. It is essentially women playing an abusive yet exciting game of locating and then treading the fine line between abandonment by the man and maintaining sadistic leverage over him through perpetual manipulation tactics. Now where this psychopathic behavior in women comes from is anyone's guess. While some may assert that it is a byproduct of the current times, there have been men acknowledging women behave in such a manner for quite a long time. While our current environment will surely play a role as well, one explanation may be that the women who were higher in the Dark Triad, and therefore not loyal to any one man or tribe, would have been more likely to live on and reproduce following tribal warfare if their tribe had lost given that the loyal women would have been reluctant to go with their captors, and likely resulting in death. Perhaps it is a mix of a number of historical/evolutionary factors and resulting in women today having developed a comfort zone around chaos as they are derived from a chain of survivors of war.

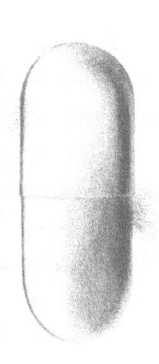

Induced Conversation

I give credit to Ross Rosenberg on YouTube for giving a name to this manipulation tactic I've observed on many occasions—what he refers to as the "narcissist's most potent weapon." His explanation is a bit different from how it played out when I observed it, so definitely check out his content for his take. This is when narcissistic people, knowing you don't want to talk, insist on talking *at you*. It is a tactic heavily based in plausible deniability: they know you don't want to talk to them but will keep attempting to make contact as though they don't. Go with your gut instinct that something feels off and don't be fooled. You will see this as well when you delete people as contacts on platforms such as Facebook: while some will come back with comments such as, "I thought we were friends," others will send you a message completely unrelated to your removing them as if they weren't aware, but you can rest assured they know, and this is why they sent the message to begin with. It's just a way to test the waters. Two observable cues that someone is aware you don't want to talk to them are that their hands shake during the interaction as well as facial expressions indicative of discomfort. It is possible as well for their voice to be a bit shaky as well as for them to engage with you in an overly positive manner coupled with a fake smile. This tactic can also be implemented on people during the *Let's Get to Know ~~Each Other~~ You phase as a desperate attempt to further datamine you for information they can use against you later.

Either You Dominate Me, Or I Dominate You

As one person put it online in comparing women's erotic literature to reality, "novel: man is a "monster"; woman is always something special, putting effort in, trying, is kind and nice, giving her best to "tame the monster." Reality: woman becomes the monster testing out the limits; man needs to come around and put her in her place." Women CRAVE dominance in men, and this may actually be the other side of what we see when men observe women: women's neotenous traits elicit a compassionate response in men, so perhaps men's masculine traits elicit a desire for dominance. This would explain women's incessant prodding of men in order to gain access to their dominant behavior; a behavior I've asserted that, if the man is not interested in responding to, becomes sexual harassment.

R.P. MENTOR TOKYO

Of course, no one is viewing women's behavior in this way, and they can use plausible deniability—their biggest weapon—to circumvent this reality if called out on it. Perhaps the woman will write her behavior off as a joke and that the target man is just "being sensitive." Moreover, there exists a narcissistic sense of entitlement to engage men in this manner wherein, if the man is not interested, women behave as though the problem is with him. From an evolutionary perspective, it makes no sense that women would predominantly be attracted to "nice guys" given that the traits which constitute this do not equate to survival or resource acquisition for children in a dangerous ancestral environment. Sure, women will pair with such men as they ensure that she has resources for the long term, but her willingness to pair with a man and what she finds sexually attractive are two different things. In accordance with what the commenter stated, this shift from the man to the woman becoming the "monster" may be a consequence of the environment having become too safe for women's primary mode of gauging men's commitment as well as ability to acquire resources (safety). Interestingly as well, a sense of fear as well as other negative emotional states elicited by interacting with a particular man may also play a role here. Perhaps a woman feels incompetent or afraid early on during their interactions. Her response may be to get over this emotional state by behaving in a disrespectful/emasculating manner in order to prove to herself that it is not warranted; and the more adamant she is about proving this to herself, the more likely she is to become a *Clinger, but this may also be due to circumstances wherein both parties are made to interact such as in a workplace. Here's an example displaying the problem with female bosses (see also Silence is ~~Golden~~ Manipulation) who have male subordinates: you're at work and request to take time off. Smirking, your boss resorts to testing to see if you will dominate her if she's provocative by making the process purposely more difficult than necessary. Perhaps she asks a question such as, do you really need to take leave right now? There is no problem nor conflicts of scheduling that would prevent this, but she is forcing you to play a dominant role with her. Notably, this is not just a behavior American women behave in. Working at a university in Japan some years ago, my boss was female with a nice-guy husband, and would insist on attempting to get me to tell her no. This was the same woman that also let me know that her biggest regret about getting married was that she didn't "try more men first," and that if I were to ask her out for a drink, she would say yes. Alternatively, of course—and I wouldn't be surprised if she had done this before—she, like any other woman can get this itch scratched by going out to locations such as bars and clubs, given that men higher in the Dark Triad frequent such locations, to facilitate their short-term mating strategy, and thus satiating a desire for dominance. I suspect the plight of modern man and woman, when it comes to what they want out of each other, goes something like as follows: Man: you have no idea how hard it is to see someone who makes you want to love and take care of them, only to be abused by them when you actually go through with it. Woman: and you have no idea how hard it is to see someone who makes you want to be controlled and dominated, only to be given care and affection when you actually engage them. In my eyes, you can display your dominance as seemingly most men and women insist on, ultimately positively reinforcing as well as informing the woman than her abusive behavior is acceptable; you can ignore it, resulting in further or even heightened testing behavior—this especially being the case if she is using sadism to be put in her place; you can confront it, likely resulting in acts such as plausible deniability or still further testing as you have no means to set boundaries (see Arguing For

Sport); or, there is another option: women desire attention and withdrawing this is tantamount to death. When women engage in testing behavior, you can cut contact.

The Trojan Horse

These are ideas passed as being to your benefit, but this is merely an attractive exterior meant to keep your guard down in order to get you to accept a likely detrimental, ulterior motive. For instance, pushback against remote workers which may have to do with managers and executives higher in the Dark Triad, especially when higher in sadism, needing factors such as narcissistic or sadistic supply. If everyone is out of the office, they can't exert their force in the same manner and adversely affect their subordinates. In looking at the arguments against masturbation, although there will be benefits to abstaining from consuming pornography, many of the proponents of this, although presenting themselves in a more altruistic light, are conveniently selling products. As was emphasized by Dr. Jordan Peterson, by engaging in this activity, men are less likely to pursue and pair with women as there is no

MANIPULATION 201

"desperation." Looking at how the marketplace is functioning today with relationships being particularly of detriment to men in multiple ways due to factors such as women's sadism, I would say that this is exactly what should occur at this point. Women, of course, also resort to shaming the act of masturbation, and unsurprisingly this is based in self-interest. One thing you'll notice is that men are shamed—by men and women alike—for behaving in a manner that goes against what women find to be in their best interest. If you don't prioritize pursuing women for sex, you're shamed for it (see Guerrilla Validation); also, if you educate yourself on women's behavior, you're shamed for it. Why would this be? Well, the way the shaming generally comes up is that you're less desirable as a man if you do this and is accompanied with smirking/laughing (see also Precarious Masculinity). Of course, what you're really doing is going against what provides women with power as they need men to over value sex in order to extract their resources. There is also no shortage of messages telling men the "masculine" thing to do is put women "in their place." Such behaviors, however, provide women with narcissistic supply through a *Power Struggle. Assertions of needing to trust people and imitation being the sincerest form of flattery comes to mind as well. In the case of the former, this message may be perpetuated by a person who has set their sights on acquiring something from you and wants you to become complacent as to make the job easier. Realistically, many relationships work in this way (see Putting Her Best Foot Forward). As for the latter, I've seen this assertion used as a way to guilt trip someone when something they've created has been plagiarized. Essentially, you should feel grateful someone is stealing from you. If there wasn't something to gain from being a proponent of these ideas, well, there wouldn't be any proponents.

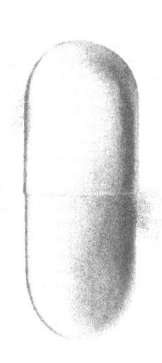

The Power Struggle

That women inherently view their interactions with men—regardless of how normal it is—as a Power Struggle, is one of the biggest red flags in my eyes. Any woman who views her interactions with a boyfriend, husband, or even acquaintance/coworker will gain a sadistic sense of joy or satisfaction in getting over on him (e.g., cheating while extracting resources); she will have no problem doing things at his expense, perhaps behaving reprehensibly while live streaming the ordeal; she will aim to get as much out of the man as possible (e.g., divorce); and this Power Struggle will last on some level from relationship start to finish, but will be the most pronounced once the woman knows she has the man's commitment on some level. Essentially having backed him into a corner, and likely increasing during the dating phase, but even more so when married. Playing on the man's masculinity will surely play a role here as women will assert that by the man not being willing to constantly fight with her—realistically, facilitating her need for a drama-rich environment—he is being "weak." As F. Roger Devlin put it, "the husband, for his part, feels like the victim of a "bait and switch" sales tactic. One wonders what would become of the human race if women told their boyfriends flat out: "you must marry me so I can stop pretending to love you as you are, and start complaining about all the ways you disappoint me." And regardless of whether you perform to the woman's narcissistic liking in dominating her, she will always view you as someone to get over on which provides her with sadistic supply, ranging anywhere from embarrassing you in public to more severe acts such as purposely sleeping with others to elicit a negative emotional response. As Dr. Sam Vaknin has shed light on, narcissists can be masochistic, so in order to obtain masochistic supply, they will use sadism. In the event you do not respond negatively to their sadistic behavior by retaliating, however, this annoys them as you are withholding supply, and so they will engage in even worse behavior—hence the progression in women's behavior over time. There are also those women who simply enjoy being sadistic for the sake of being sadistic, and so they can engage in covert acts that they either keep to themselves or gossip about with

MANIPULATION 201

friends afterwards as entertainment. Interestingly, and likely throwing many men off, they're essentially damned if they do and damned if they don't behave dominantly: let's say you have a more compassionate man in a relationship who wants to treat who he perceives as his partner well. By doing this, she lashes out at him with abuse. He then resorts to behaving a bit more dominantly and significantly less caring towards the woman as he begins to pick up on this mode of interaction perhaps being more so what she wants. The woman does become a bit less abusive, but this has been replaced with complaining about the behavior. So, the man is confused, and cuts back on some of his newly implemented behaviors only for the woman to lash out with abuse like before. It would seem that such a plight serves as a test of sorts wherein he is forced into a dominant role, but regardless of how the man treats the woman, all she expresses is a negative emotional state—a trait found in narcissists. If he is compassionate, he is dominated; if he is dominant, the woman plays on his proclivity to be compassionate which dominates his dominant behavior as he doesn't want to treat the woman badly. The only way this dynamic works is if the man is higher in the Dark Triad wherein only the dominant/uncompassionate side is harbored. In my eyes, it is no wonder relations just don't work, and in the case of this persistence by women to attempt to force men to satiate their desire for dominance as well as a drama-rich environment—even in the most mundane of situations wherein it is not at all necessary such as the workplace (see Either You Dominate Me, Or I Dominate You)—well, you can be "masculine," and put a woman "in her place," *or*, you can just cut contact—cutting off her narcissistic supply. Narcissists enjoy arguing, so trying to set boundaries by acknowledging what you don't like and telling them to stop is not going to work as it is actually an enjoyable experience for the woman. In fact, your bringing attention to certain behaviors will be memorized as specifically how to bother you in the future. Furthermore, the narcissist is never going to stop pushing the man's boundaries but will find different ways to do so which the man will spend the rest of his days calling them out on. The compassion gap between the sexes can be understood from multiple perspectives: (1) in the case of the evolutionary, that it would be safer for women to not become attached to a particular man due in part to a dangerous ancestral environment meaning a high chance of his passing. (2) When considering instances of women being taken as tribal war prizes for reproductive purposes, it would also have been more advantageous to harbor a psychology that was less loyal to any one man or even tribe given that to be loyal would likely mean death in the event she fought against the winners of war. And (3), in simply observing the enjoyment they get, albeit covertly, from behaving horribly towards men in general. Regardless of which way you look at it, it is apparent that women lack compassion for men, and you can observe this even in instances wherein a man had a horrible upbringing, the woman is aware of it, and still resorts to sadistic testing behavior. Of course, you can write this off as some form of autopilot meant to ensure women survive to reproduce, but this doesn't negate the fact that women's compassion for men—regardless of how much they may fake it—is nonexistent. And regardless of the background psychological mechanisms at play which facilitate these tendencies in women, there are post-hoc rationalizations at play. Likely a sadistic sense of enjoyment from getting away with behaviors that adversely affect those around them as there are no consequences which positively reinforces their negative behaviors. To judge people's compassion for others, it is commonly suggested to observe their interactions with those they don't have anything to gain from, such as a waiter/waitress. Sadly, when it comes to women's behavior towards men, it seems this piece of advice has been completely forgotten. I think F. Roger Devlin puts it well in stating that "the misguided gallantry of the typical male pundit may to some extent simply be a component of male heterosexuality: since men naturally desire women, they have a vested interest in believing women worth having."

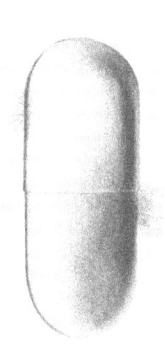

Indirect Questions

Women's sadistic game of *Monkey in the Middle may involve indirectly asking questions about committed manipulative acts to see if you have picked up on them. You are considered "weak" if you do not satiate women's desire for a drama-rich environment which the game provides, and in the event you express that they are bothering you, they behave as though the problem is with you and continue to behave in a sadistic manner. An example of using indirect questions goes as follows: in the office, a coworker asserting while slightly laughing, that she had to stay late due to the boss calling her for a meeting at the end of day and asks if you had noticed that the boss engages in this behavior. This question is meant to establish a false sense of rapport with laughter as well as a having a common negative experience when, in all actuality, she did not experience this but is aware it has happened to you. She wants you to feel comfortable enough to gossip with her about a person she is perhaps colluding with, but surely trying to get in the good graces of. In the case of collusion, the boss may have asked this co-worker to ask the question. As for the co-worker trying to get in the boss's good graces, they may have observed similar behavior by the boss, and are now trying to get you to speak badly about them to report anything negative you say. Ultimately, the goal of getting you to gossip about the other person is to get you to expose information that can be used against you. Additionally, such fuel can serve the function of isolating you: what you say is reported to the third party—in this case, the boss—either making them not like you when the co-worker is trying to get in the boss's good graces, and/or satiating a sadistic drive when the co-worker and boss are colluding with each other. The former can lead to the latter as the manipulator first gets the boss to dislike you and then they collude with each other against you. In the case of the former as well, people don't inquire whether this information is true as they tend to assume that the first thing they hear is correct, so while you're getting the cold shoulder from people or they just act strangely towards you, the manipulator can be perceived of as the only person close to you as they purposely isolated you. Indirect statements are also leveraged when manipulators assume they hold information about you that you are unaware of so they can observe your responses to them. This can be used to elicit negative emotional responses as well as just for entertainment. For instance, perhaps someone learns about a secret of yours or something negative that happened to you. As gossip or snooping has allowed the manipulator to learn this information about you, they may bring it up indirectly or as happening to someone else. In order to get you more invested in the conversation, they may resort to asking you questions aimed at obtaining information such as what you would do in such a situation. This is yet another sadistic tactic as, not only does this serve to elicit a negative emotional response, but they can simultaneously gather more information, check if the source of gossip was correct, and all the while feel superior in knowing that you won't come forward about your own experience. Of course, in the event you do, plausible deniability will be used to maintain the perception of being oblivious. Furthermore, if you do come forward with this information, it is just used as an invitation to pry for further information.

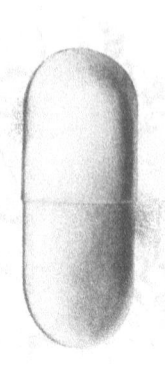

Do You Think They Noticed?

Manipulators, when they suspect you're onto them, can respond in different ways. One of the easier ones to pinpoint is them reaching out to you. Take for instance a situation wherein you notice that someone has been stealing from you. To get a gauge of where your mind is at on the subject, the culprit may be one of the first people to get in contact with you. This will especially be the case if they are a *Clinger: while they are actively taking from you, they additionally have plans to exploit you in the future, so they need to ensure that you are not suspicious of them. This tendency by manipulators can also pop up when you publicly post about something indirectly related to their behavior. Take for instance a scenario wherein you make a social-media post about a certain negative behavior or trait (e.g., narcissism) which is characteristic of the manipulator, but not necessarily directed at them as you're educating yourself on the subject. Commonly, they will be one of the first people to like the post or leave a response message.

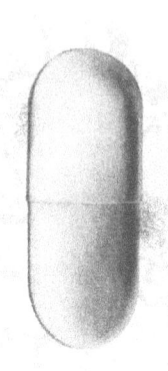

Precarious Masculinity

This is when outside parties—generally women—will assert a particular trait or behavior is "masculine" or the "masculine thing to do." In reality, however, this is yet another case of language used as a means-to-an-end strategy in eliciting a desired emotional/behavioral response. If they can get you to adopt and furthermore engage in behaviors they find to be in their best interest by reinforcing them under the guise of "masculinity," they can mold you in whatever way they find most beneficial to their own goals. This can be anything from paying for extravagant first dates (see The Tradwife Con) to enduring their psychopathic as well as abusive testing behavior (see The Power Struggle).

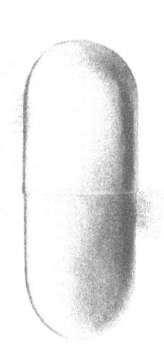

Living Rent Free in Your Head

Women, as with the Maroon 5 song, "don't care what you think as long as it's about" them. And while "the best of" women "can find happiness in misery" through pursuing retaliation from men due to their bad behavior, that they think this behavior brings men closer to them shows that they are blindly projecting. In the same manner that eliciting strong emotional responses plays a significant role in men's success when pursuing women, women will project this strategy as effective onto men. It is competing to take up space in the man's mind: as they themselves feed off of emotional responses and view, like publicity, the negative to be better than none when it comes to the emotional responses they elicit in men—today, more emphasis being placed on the negative—they use this in the same manner as is effectively used on them. That is to say, while some women may enjoy receiving backhanded compliments, men find this kind of behavior from women less than desirable. In fact, many would not use this strategy at all if it did not work. When this fails, however, women go on to repeat this process; in some cases, perhaps doubling down in order to leave their mark so that they are thought of by the man regardless. Remember, narcissists assume that everyone's psychology functions like theirs, so projection is par for the course.

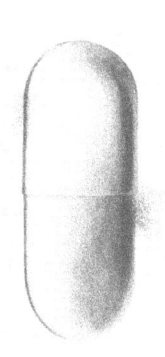

You Got Me Pregnant!

Pregnancy scares, whether legitimate or otherwise, are one of the biggest, and sadly it seems, effective methods of women's pseudo-hypoagency. Hypoagency, as Karen Straughan has talked about, comes down to women viewing themselves as objects in the world who are acted upon instead of actors who make things happen. By the woman getting you to believe that you are solely responsible for the pregnancy—as if she wasn't present throughout the sex act—she is implementing pseudo-hypoagency as she is knowingly leveraging this object status in the hopes of the man taking full responsibility for this "unfortunate" and/or "distressing" set of circumstances. This quite obviously plays to her benefit as this tactic would only be used on a man she sees benefit in forcing/tricking into a long-term relationship. Men are already prone toward facilitating women's hypoagency as many do not view them as actors to begin with, and this is likely in part due to their neotenous traits. Women, on some level, are aware of this and can use this to their advantage here. It's all about the effective extraction of resources and the target's masculinity may also be called into question if he does not provide her access to them (see Precarious Masculinity for an explanation of this). The woman may genuinely be pregnant at the time of asserting that the man is to blame; however, plausible deniability can also be used here as, in the event the man takes responsibility, the woman now knows that she has control of the situation. If she is not really pregnant, she can now initiate sex with the man in order to purposely cause the situation she blamed the man for to begin with. So, fake the pregnancy to test the commitment waters; in the even the man goes along with it, purposely get pregnant; but if he declines, shame him to the extent he is found valuable. This process furthermore serves to test not only how committed the target man is, but how compassionate: during this process of revealing the supposed circumstances, the woman will likely feign genuine signs of emotions such as fear, being distraught, confused, sadness—perhaps even crying—and of course victimhood as well as uncertainty regarding what she's going to do. The woman is implementing these emotional signs to gauge, as she has been throughout the duration of the relationships, how compassionate the man is which plays to her benefit when it comes to selecting a long-term partner. This parallels women's assertion that a particular sexual position hurts to a man she is vetting as a long-term partner as, in the event he backs off—notably, a position she has likely enjoyed with Dark Triad men who are not compassionate, and thus, she harbors sexual desire for—she knowns she can manipulate him through this facet of his psychology.

The Tradwife Con

As I detailed in *The "Where Have All the Good Men Gone?" Hypothesis*, a shift in the gender-academic gap played a significant role in women not finding men in their available mating pool to be desirable. Today we have many women prioritizing their careers first, but then abruptly shifting to prioritizing securing a long-term provider after leading a life revolving around a short-term mating strategy (i.e., hookups). Interestingly, in their younger years, some of these women engage in manipulative behavior to con men out of their resources which I refer to as The Tradwife Con. This is a mix of what has commonly been referred to as the "foodie call," essentially going out on dates with men for the sole purpose of getting free food, with presenting an exaggerated facade of traditional values in a plausibly deniable self-serving manner so as to persuade the man to feel comfortable in investing in her. This works because men will falsely assume that the woman has genuine traditional values, and therefore, that he is investing in a woman who is relationship oriented, but this could not be farther from the case. In considering that women's short-term mating strategy consists of not only prioritizing looks, but the man providing her resources up front, you can use this information to your advantage if you are a man who is relationship minded. That is to say, if a woman is insisting that you wine and dine her during a first date, and especially if she is averse to engaging in any activity that actually prioritizes getting to know you as a person, take this as a sign that she may be engaging in a short-term mating strategy and has no intention of investing in you. Of course, women will continue to insist that this is their minimum standard for dating today in attempts at further normalizing the exploitation of men.

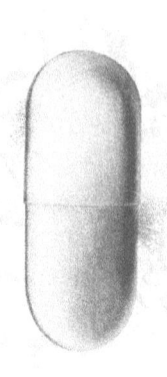

Putting Her Best Food Forward

Falsely advertising oneself from the outset of a potential relationship is a common as well as accepted strategy in acquiring a partner, but of course, this is engaged in to differing extents. The problem comes in for men when women portray themselves to such a false extent from the start, gain the man's commitment, and then begin to withdraw the positive qualities the man appreciated which tied him into the relationship to begin with. An example of this can come in the form of a woman initiating conversations she assumes the man is interested in—commonly based on stereotypes, but the woman may also have researched the man prior—so as to present herself as a more viable partner. This furthermore serves to circumvent the phase of getting to know the other person as their interests were never important to begin with. What *is* important, however, is getting her foot in the door in order to extract

MANIPULATION 201

whatever desired resource(s) the man possesses (e.g., status, money, etc.). Women know that they need to behave in a certain manner to lock down a man. In considering that her actions up to this point may have predominantly been based around hook ups, this of course, will have the consequence of certain modes of interaction conducive to this lifestyle being ingrained. Due to this, she will need to sell herself by putting her best foot forward or wearing a mask as to reflect what she perceives the man is looking for in a long-term partner. Notably, this isn't much of a problem for many women given that they're much more in tune with factors such as nonverbal cues, but also, if they are higher in the Dark Triad, they are quite skilled at reading people which directly facilitates knowing how to exploit them. One problem with this tactic, however, is that a mask can only be kept on for so long, but if she is successful, and manages to get her foot in the door, there is the potential for this strategy to result in marriage wherein she feels comfortable completely taking it off as the man is in a compromised position. I view this dynamic as something akin to the act of a grocery store placing new expiration dates on expiring or already expired products. In both cases, the ultimate goal is a self-serving one wherein extending the product's shelf life in attempts at making a sale through acts of manipulation take priority over the wellbeing of the buyer who is simply viewed as a resource in the equation. Although the buyer may not be aware that the product is expired at the time of purchase, with time, they may be made aware either upon opening the product (i.e., living with and observing the woman's actions), during consumption (i.e., her generating a bad taste in the man's mouth), or even later on by some form of adverse health reaction (e.g., psychological due to acts stemming from her emotional baggage/abuse or even a disease due to her reverting back to a short-term mating strategy). Notably, and perhaps, unfortunately, in the case of the latter of these, the buyer may not associate this reaction with the product, and so an alternative rationalization may take the blame if anything at all.

I Just Need to Try Harder

As men tend to be problem solvers as well as take responsibility, they may resort to thinking that they just need to try harder or that they are to blame for the woman's shift in behavior, when in all actuality, the woman is manipulating him. Perhaps she will *Complain in Order to Maintain him. This is another case wherein a sadistic aspect may exist as the woman gets enjoyment out of observing the man try harder—resulting in her garnering more of his resources—as well as seeing how unpleasantly she can treat the man with him continuing to stay. The woman may very well be a *Clinger who, upon the man deciding to end the relationship, pretends that she has magically come to realize that her behavior over the course of the relationship was wrong, and now she is ready to change for the better. Of course, if the man does take her back, she will quickly revert to her old ways.

DESTROY ME!

For women who perceive that they have wronged their partner, they may provoke their partner on purpose to the point of them retaliating against them in order to feel as though they are even. Of course, the man has no idea why this is occurring, but by getting him to respond to her provocative behavior, she can feel as though she's not the only one in the wrong, and therefore allowing her to feel as though she's not as bad of a person. In some cases, the woman will establish a risk-averse scenario wherein the man's behavior is directed by the woman. One such example can be found in the book, *Why Women Have Sex*, by Drs. Cindy Meston and David Buss: a girl hurt her boyfriend emotionally, so she directed his positioning during sex in a manner that would hurt her. The purpose of this was to allow her to feel better about herself without actually addressing the problem with her then partner. It is an interesting rationalization process, and this particular girl in retrospect, stated that she "thought" that her partner knew something was wrong. Of course, this could just be a self-serving post-hoc rationalization which allows her to falsely perceive that she has set the records straight. Such a process allows women who engage in bad behavior, wherein their partner faces some form of negative consequence, to view unilaterally deciding how things will be handled instead of addressing their behavior with their partner as a viable, although ultimately risk averse, option. Analogy: a woman steals money from her boyfriend. The boyfriend required this money to afford medication, and as a consequence of this theft, had to undergo an amputation—essentially losing something he will never get back much in the same way as one may commit to actions that lose a partner's trust in a relationship. The girlfriend can obviously see the consequences of her bad behavior, and instead of engaging with the boyfriend directly, risk aversely resorts to taking a portion of the money she stole and mailing it back to him. She doesn't bother putting her name on the envelope, but in her self-serving rationalization process, convinces herself that the boyfriend knew it was her sending the money. Upon sending the envelope, she feels a bit better about herself, that things are a bit more even, and therefore absolving herself of guilt despite the remaining damage the boyfriend must deal with as a consequence of her actions.

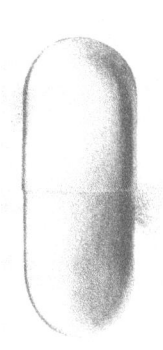

Not All Women Are Like That

This is a form of gaslighting which can serve to keep men perpetually pursuing women with the false idea that, despite the commonality of women's bad behavior, the next one will be better—or even, the right one. One thing you'll notice is that men are shamed—by men and women alike—for behaving in a manner that goes against what women find to be in their best interest. If you don't prioritize sex, you're shamed for it; if you educate yourself on women's behavior, you're shamed for it. Why would this be? Well, the way this shaming is generally expressed is that you're less desirable as a man if you engage in such behaviors and is accompanied by smirking/laughing. Of course, what you're really doing is going against what provides women with power as they need men to over-value sex in order to extract resources. Moreover, when these attempts in shaming fail—forcing manipulators to focus on the realities of the relationship between men and women—anger is a common response (see The Truth in Anger); and the closer you get to the truth, the stronger this response. To admit that women are a certain way, in the case of women, is to admit how they themselves are. In the case of men, and especially if they have internalized how women are, it is to acknowledge that they may have wasted a significant amount of their life. As F. Roger Devlin stated, "many men continue to insist, in defiance of all the evidence of women's actual behavior, that they are pining away for morally upright men to love, honor, and obey, and that the poor dears cannot find happiness only because other men (never the writer himself, of course) are selfish, irresponsible cads."

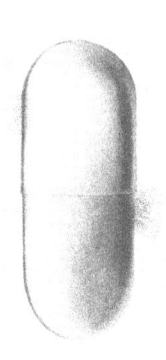

Complain to Maintain

While it is the case that many women will complain as they feel entitled to have men do more for them despite providing significantly less, the act of complaining may also be leveraged in order to redirect the man's attention from this discrepancy in value. As Dr. David Buss stated, "when tactics such as providing resources, love, and kindness fail, people sometimes resort to desperate emotional tactics to retain their mates, particularly if they are lower in mate value." To this, I would say that many women will completely skip this "providing" stage and jump to "emotional tactics to retain their mates" as they inherently view their interactions with men as a *Power Struggle. Whether it be a grandiose woman or otherwise, the goal is to continue her steady flow of incoming resources. The underlying mindset may be one based in fear: the woman is afraid the man will realize she is getting the better deal, and especially, again, as she views the relationship as a *Power Struggle. Due to this, complaining is used to make it appear as though the man is not doing enough, which is internalized by the man as he is the lucky one in the relationship. Women's ability to get men to think they are getting the better deal is compounded by the fact that, even at the initial stages of interaction, many of them feign disinterest. Of course, in many cases this will be completely true as they are not physically attracted to the man but will feign interest as they are covertly pursuing the man's resources. One such instance I've observed firsthand of this behavior was when a female coworker with narcissistic as well as psychopathic tendencies asserted that her husband needed to do more for her. Not long before this, however, she had admitted that she was not particularly good at anything. As narcissism is a compensatory psychological condition, this makes sense.

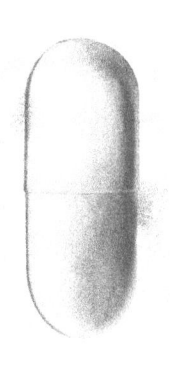

Condition+Phobic=SHAME ON YOU!

You've likely heard assertions—commonly from women—that men are perhaps commitment phobic or even fat phobic. This is yet another case of language used as a means-to-an-end strategy in eliciting a desired emotional/behavioral response in men. How this works is the assertion is presented as being based in morality (i.e., you hate fat/trans women) or plays on masculinity (e.g., "you're just afraid to get hurt" or "who hurt you?"), but ultimately is meant to fulfil the self-serving purpose of getting the man to, well, "man up," and provide the manipulator with his resources. This strategy is an attempt at circumventing the marketplace dynamic of supply and demand: consumers desire specific products; in this case, not what the accuser is selling, so they resort to attempting to shame consumers into buying it anyway. Essentially, shame on you for not permitting the manipulator(s) to garner your resources by buying their product (i.e., the manipulator which expands their mating/partnering pool).

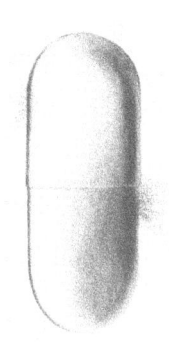

Clingers

These are "friends" who will cling onto you and can even appear to legitimately be on your side in using tactics such as *Let's Get to Know ~~Each Other~~ You. You may even notice these people providing positive feedback about whatever you're pursuing, but in all actuality, they are adamant about maintaining contact as they perceive that you will be able to provide them with some form of desired resource in the future (e.g., a job opportunity) and additionally may have it in their mind that they will negatively impact your life. Once they have acquired this desired resource, their friendly demeanor may come to an end, but not around you. This parallels with two of the corollaries to Dr. Robert Briffault's law:

1. Regardless of how much you've helped a woman in the past, it constitutes no guarantee for the continuation of the relationship in the future.

2. A woman's promise to continue a relationship based around some form of resource becomes null as soon as said resource has been obtained.

Clingers can actually be rather jealous of and/or even resent you, and a simple way to test this (see also The Golden Rule) is to observe their facial expression when you state something positive going on in your life. If it elicits a facial expression indicative of being upset or angry, this is not someone you want around. Do keep in mind that this shift in facial expression can also occur when you, perhaps, mention something you enjoyed such as a television show, etc. Clingers may insist on complimenting or even hugging you which can, and is likely meant, to throw you off their trail while they bide their time. There can be a sense of fakeness to their interaction style as it seems forced, and it is. Take for instance a woman who constantly compliments a man who focuses on content about women's negative impact on men. She is likely maintaining contact as a means to an end; if there was nothing to gain from the man, there would be no point in complimenting his work which actually elicits a negative emotional response in her. Clingers can also feel entitled to your time—insisting on initiating conversations they find to be to their benefit, and when you don't perform to their liking, this may also elicit a negative facial expression. In this sense, they are heavily narcissistic. Clingers, whether in, or outside of a relationship context, may perceive that you have wronged them at some point whether you are aware of it or not and/or are sadistic, resulting in them behaving horribly in attempts at getting back at you, enjoying the process (sadism), but attempting to hide it. This may manifest as a woman who sleeps with her "partner's" friends with all parties involved keeping it a secret—perhaps even as an inside joke. Notably, women's insistence on pursuing men higher in socioeconomic status comes along with the added benefit of easily being able to transition to one of the man's friends who is of equal, but preferably, higher status. This is another reason they may insist—perhaps saying something along the lines of "you never introduce me to your friends" and accompanied by a smirk—on becoming intertwined in your friend group. To test for sadism, do the opposite of the last test: observe their facial expression when you state something *negative* going on in your life. If it elicits a facial expression indicative of experiencing joy such as a smirk or even them quickly attempting to hide their face, again, this is not someone you want around, but lucky you as you spotted the clinger. In the event you find out about at least one of their acts against you (e.g., infidelity) and end the relationship, they may feign remorse to pull you back in for further manipulation and abuse. This is a state of affairs seemingly the majority of men have gone through wherein their "partner" is abusive towards them throughout the relationship, they decide to end things, and suddenly the woman expresses signs of remorse—perhaps purposely crying which, I find it worth noting here that women have more narrow tear ducts. This means that learning to cry during childhood is much easier for them on a physiological level, but also because only boys are punished for expressing sadness in this manner. As displaying sadness through crying works to their benefit in eliciting a highly compassionate response in observers, it should come as no surprise that this natural ability becomes a rather honed skill over the years and can be used against you as it likely was with her father as well as other men throughout their lives. Narcissistic people will surely be prone to this behavior as they project their own manipulative tendencies onto others as if the way their psychology functions is universal. It is also worth noting that Clingers may cling to each other in forming a group for purposes such as initiating a game of *Monkey in the Middle. While peer pressure may play a role in this clinging of Clingers, resulting in perhaps one member not actually being a Clinger initially, but is converted into one if not just as a byproduct of peer pressure, the group may harbor a shared resentment for you. Not necessarily for anything you did, or at least, intended to do to them, but how they perceived your actions—likely as a consequence of projection—and any negative emotional responses they elicited. Needless to say, it is necessary to discard of Clingers as soon as possible as they will attempt to cling to you for as long as they see benefit in doing so—even if just for satiating a sadistic drive by acts such as smiling in your face while sabotaging you. In the event you do manage to spot and discard a Clinger, however, they may still try to sabotage, or at least keep tabs on you indirectly through mutual friends and even through means such as tracking your online profiles such as LinkedIn to spread false information to future employers.

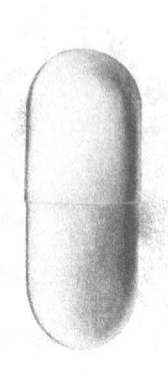

Misery Loves Company

Unfortunately, it seems that the underlying mentality harbored by many people who, perhaps, followed the herd, or followed a path they are not happy with, is to get *you* to go down that path as well. Essentially, it is a mindset of compensation: if I had to go through this, so do you. We commonly see this with married men who insist on the single men around them following in their footsteps despite how obviously discontent they are with how their lives turned out. Similarly, this state of affairs can be observable when it comes to women who prioritized hookups in their youth, only to abruptly shift their mindset to wanting to become a housewife after over a decade of not practicing any of the necessary skills to fulfil this role for a man. At this point, the woman's ship had likely sailed years prior—surely having discarded a suitable partner or two along the way—so she doubles down by telling younger women not of her mistakes, but that she is proud of who she has become, and that these young women should enjoy their youth and "discover themselves" (i.e., sleep around). Whether it be men or women who, in retrospect, realize that they may have made some mistakes, they want to be compensated for going through it as well as not feel as though they made a bad decision; and what better way to accomplish this than to get everyone on the same boat as themselves. Dr. Robert Briffault interestingly quoted a Mr. Rockhill in stating that "by what means have those women gained such complete ascendancy over the men, how have they made their mastery so complete and so acceptable to a race of lawless barbarians who but unwillingly submit to the authority of their chiefs, is a problem well worth consideration." While we cannot be completely certain as to how this took place historically, today I can provide an answer to at least some extent: Misery Loves Company. Men's egotism as well as desire for being compensated for what they went through contributes to women's "ascendancy." As much as it may seem that I have some form of rare insight into women's behavior, while being on the spectrum of autism may have aided me in picking up on some trends, I don't buy into the idea that I'm special in having pinpointed their negative behaviors. In the same manner that South Korean males would try to push others—mind you, this is in childhood—to go through with circumcision right after they had undergone the procedure, and this persists throughout adulthood, I think we're looking at the same thing here with men remaining somewhat oblivious to how disappointing relationships can be until they're in the thick of it. Men get taken advantage of or endure some unfortunate event(s), and instead of aiding other men to not end up in the same boat as them—for instance, marriage—they will try to push you to walk the same path. Misery loves company, so why not stay a while? Better yet, I'll convince others to repeat this unfortunate cycle so I don't feel as bad about my past decisions. Do realize that you *are* alone in this world, with few exceptions, and regardless of how giving people—in many cases, *Clingers—may present themselves to be.

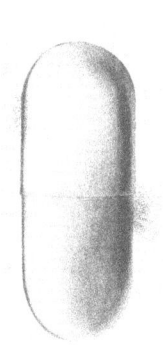

Arguing For Sport

As effective as women's facial expressions can be on men due in part to their neotenous facial features, but also that the man may just not want people to feel negatively, it becomes rather easy for women to purposely initiate arguments. All she has to do is feign being upset or angry, and the man is likely to engage her as though her emotional responses are genuine. Women are well aware of this and will argue for purposes such as seeing if they can beat the man as a form of entertainment. As is the case with narcissists, women enjoy arguing in general, and ultimately end up wasting everyone's time present as they will argue a point they know is incorrect for the sake of arguing. Notably, attempting to set boundaries in the form of telling them to stop a certain behavior is ultimately pointless as this is found to be an enjoyable experience and is followed by shifting their behavior to make you tell them to stop for the duration of your relationship with them. This form of testing, just like the others, serves the additional function of keeping the focus on themselves for as long as possible. This is why arguing with many women is pointless: it is a game of, *I will only concede on topics you can back me into a corner on, despite knowing that I was wrong from the start*. Similarly, you have people in comments sections purposely saying things obviously wrong or provocative for the sake of being provocative. These tend to be narcissistic baiting strategies meant to start an argument as well as see how much attention they can garner, whether positive or negative, as there is a strong need for relevance. It is something akin to a child's mindset that says, "chase me, play with me." Similarly, and as an example of how adamant women can be in pursuing drama as well as feeling a sense of superiority through manipulation, following my setting a no-contact rule at a previous job with a particular female employee, she resorted to reopening cabinets I had recently closed in the hopes of getting me to close them again. It is rather interesting how obsessed women can be in their pursuit of relevancy as well as *Living in Your Head Rent Free, but this is of course permitted as there are no consequences for their actions. As many men may think that this kind of behavior is culturally bound (i.e., only in the west), this is far from the case: even here in Japan, one outlet you'll find for this need to establish a *Power Struggle, manipulate, and pursue dominant behavior can commonly be observed through women who purposely walk on the wrong side of the street where men are walking. Imagine that you're walking on the left side of the street while the oncoming traffic uses the right side. Some Japanese women will elect to walk on the left side—even spotting you ahead of time when your head is down and walking directly at you—which initiates a sort of game of chicken. In one particular instance that comes to mind, I kept my eyes on the face of a particular woman that was obviously on the wrong side walking towards me and noticed a rather large smirk on her face in passing. As Dr. Robert Briffault even observed, "in the province of Dongola, the position of the husband is equally abject. His relations with his wife are carefully regulated by tribal law…"Further, he should bear with all her caprices, or if she abuses him, he is expected to laugh at it and is not despised for so doing. The husband is absolutely forbidden to beat his wife, whatever her offence."

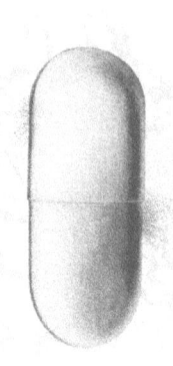

Silence is ~~Golden~~ Manipulation

This is a tactic which some people use through speech but also text. They will pretend to make a big deal about a simple situation and ask why you, perhaps, think a certain way or changed your mind on something. After asking this question, they will use silence to their benefit as the other party will generally feel uncomfortable in this silence, coupled with being stared at, and feel inclined to provide a long explanation while acquiescing to the other person. This allows the manipulative party to gain a sense of power over the target. An example of this can go as follows: you're at work and you disagree with taking on a particular task, so you voice this. Your boss who initially tasked you asks, "what do you mean? Why aren't you doing this task?", in a seemingly serious manner while starting at you. You provide an explanation, inquiring if they insist that you take on the task. The boss quickly smiles, then drops the whole situation.

Let's Get to Know ~~Each Other~~ You

It is a commonly known red flag for people to insist on you disclosing more intimate details about yourself early on, but nonetheless, you will run into people who implement this strategy. Women asserting that men just need to "open up" is nothing new as it is to their benefit to get men to do so for various reasons. They may bombard you with questions early on and insist on spending copious amounts of time together with the goal of gaining as much information as possible. Narcissists amongst other people will engage with you in this manner as, the more information on you they have, the more they can mold themselves into a person you perceive as a great match or desirable person to be around. This same strategy in establishing false rapport can furthermore be implemented in order to pinpoint where you are the most vulnerable—what the manipulator will perceive as weak points. By learning where you are vulnerable, they gain power. An example of this would be someone who discloses that they were bullied as a child, but in all actuality, they were the bully. The other person opens up about how they have had similar experiences, and as they took the manipulator's words as genuine, proceeds to open up about exactly how they used to be bullied in the past. The manipulator then stores this information for future use—perhaps implementing plausibly deniable variants of the style of bullying they experienced in the past given that where trauma lies tends to leave people open to further exploitation. Likely there will be a sadistic aspect to all of this as the manipulator gets enjoyment out of deceiving and abusing the target. Notably as well, this is a strategy women commonly use with men in relationships: they will insist that the target man open up, and once he does, this information he provides will be used against him in the future. And men, again directly facilitating women's hypoagency, will insist that these women don't know any better when they engage in overt abusive behaviors.

Guerrilla Validation

I think this is a rather common one that you may have come across. Guerrilla Validation is when people insist and even go as far as to shaming as well as harassing you in order to adopt some activity or value that they hold with high regard. By getting you to adopt what they value, it provides them with a sense of superiority as once this shift occurs, they perceive that it puts them above you, and this is due in part to them having heavily invested in it. This, however, is not possible if you do not value what they do. For example, let's say you are out with a guy at a bar who overly values pursuing women. The reason you decided to come out was just to relax; however, he insists that you blindly pursue (see Throw Him to the Wolves) just as he does, which is an activity that he has invested copious amounts of time engaging in and perhaps even studying. You display little interest in this, and so he resorts to shaming you—even going so far as to attempting to get other people in the bar to join in on this. Perhaps he'll even insist that you think you're special because you don't need to pursue women. Notably, there will be a sadistic aspect to this behavior in that a sense of accomplishment is elicited from getting you to acquiesce to their demands as well as the shaming of their recruited outside parties leading to converting you; but also in observing you fail if this does occur as it further allows them to feel superior. They are forcing you into a competition that they perceive they will ultimately win. If you do succeed in the manipulator's valued activity of choice (e.g., pursuing women, video games, etc.), however, it is not uncommon for them to try and sabotage you. For instance, if you finally throw your hands up and acquiesce to their insistence that you pursue women and are actually successful in doing so—especially if it is to an extent that displays possessing more skill than the manipulator—they may resort to acts such as talking badly about you to the women in order to sabotage you—proving, albeit dishonestly, to themselves that they are superior. This is a highly narcissistic trait based in a *Power Struggle.

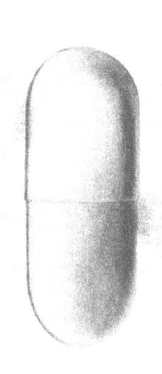

DON'T TAKE THE BAIT!

It is true that the negative sticks out in people's minds more than the positive which is why it has been said that it takes more positive instances in a relationship to undo the negative feelings brought about by a bad one. Whether consciously or not, people such as narcissists have exploited this ingrained tendency in people online, and to great effect. You can commonly observe people in comments sections purposely saying things obviously wrong or provocative for the sake of being provocative which is a narcissistic baiting strategy meant to start an argument, or at the least, draw some kind of attention to themselves. You may have even felt compelled to respond to such comments only to be met rather quickly with an argumentative response. DON'T TAKE THE BAIT, not even when you see this in the comments section of my videos as you're providing the commenter exactly what they want: narcissistic supply through attention whether it be positive *or* negative. Notably, women function in this manner as well given that they crave attention, and therefore they will take positive as well as negative attention. Narcissistic people enjoy arguing which allows them to feel relevant even if only to observe that their words *do* have an effect on you. In the case of women who are invited onto the more popular podcast panels today, they implement the same strategy: to keep the attention on themselves for as long as possible, they resort to wasting everyone's time present by arguing points they knew were wrong from the start in order to keep the host talking, but also to observe their emotional response—perhaps dominant (attractive), but also negative (sadism). This is why arguing with narcissists as well as many women is pointless as it is a game of, I will only concede on topics you can back me into a corner on, despite knowing that I was wrong from the start. Again, DON'T TAKE THE BAIT! I may even start typing "bait" as a response to comments I suspect fall under this manipulation tactic.

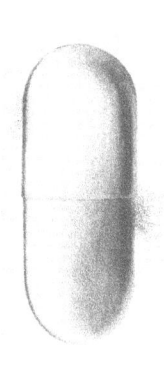

Pseudo-Projection

This is a plausibly deniable assertion based in manipulation, and in many cases, serves to guilt trip the target or shift their perception of reality in a self-serving manner. To use the lonely-old-man myth, in the case of regular projection, the woman asserts that the man will be lonely if he doesn't pair with someone—more specifically her, but not phrased as such—but this is merely a manifestation of her own desires and/or fears. Essentially, she may on some level believe that his value system functions in this way, but unbeknownst to her, it is merely projection. Alternatively, in the case of women's common assertion that men desire pushback, like that of the extrovert asserting that they just need to get an introvert "out of their shell," is likely borne out of both projection as well as post-hoc rationalizations. These are rationalizations brought about by one's inherent traits, and conveniently, they reinforce actions they find to be in their own best interest. In both cases, it's not that their behavior is undesirable—which seemingly never even registers—but that they are actually being helpful or doing the other person a favor. In the extrovert's eyes, the introvert will be better off after they push them to be more like themselves, but this is ultimately to convert the introvert into a source of attention—a desired resource. These desires are so strong that even in the face of negative responses upon engaging in these behaviors (e.g., introvert becomes annoyed), they may not hinder them from attempting to satiate their drives by these means in the future. Not only this, but the original assertion that the other party desires this, and therefore, that they're doing them a favor, will likely persist as well. Essentially, people will rationalize the means by which they satiate their drives, and although outside parties serve as a resource in this equation, an altruistic narrative serves to preemptively mitigate the chances of the onset of cognitive dissonance. To use the example of the lonely-old-man myth in the case of Pseudo-Projection, however, the woman is fully aware of the difference between her value system and that of the man's. As the target man would be one with many options, perhaps higher in the Dark Triad, and therefore unlikely to settle down, the goal here would be to test to see if she can plant a seed of fear in his mind for his future which benefits her in the event she can get him to change his mating strategy for her. Ultimately, however, the woman is viewing the target man as a source of untapped resources consciously or unconsciously, and considering women's in-group bias—termed in research as "implicit bias"—this may serve to provide herself or another woman with them (see Man: The Untapped Resource). This of course could also be the case with women who assert that men desire pushback: as women commonly view their interactions with men as a *Power Struggle, while this could be a consequence of them projecting their desire for a drama-rich environment onto the man, there surely will be other women implementing Pseudo-Projection in that they are well aware that men have no interest in pushback, but assert this anyway, perhaps in attempts at normalizing their behavior.

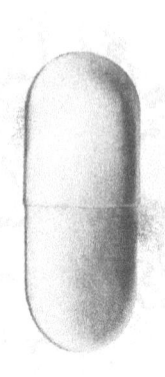

Man: The Untapped Resource

There are surely many reasons why any information—whether based in fact or not—that goes against the idea that men *need* to pair with women will never go mainstream, and regardless of the common consequences for doing so (e.g., negative health outcomes, etc.). While relationships, like constantly being around people in general, is not for everyone, people will assert that it is the answer for all men. If you notice, however, the people making these assertions tend to have something to gain from trying to change your mind. This being whether it is a woman who wants you to provide her or other women with your resources, men who need you to value what they do to validate themselves or desire compensation (see Guerrilla Validation and Misery Loves Company), or those who want to sell you a product. For example, in accordance with women's in-group bias, a woman who is looking for a hookup

MANIPULATION 201

and isn't hurting for resources at the time, in speaking with a safer and less exciting man, may resort to attempting to introduce him to a friend who is a single mother. Women want to keep as many men in their available pool of prospective partners as it ensures that they always have available resources; and they become quite curious, in some cases even upset/angry (see The Truth in Anger), when a man displays disinterest in availing himself to women in this manner. In these instances, they commonly resort to asking exactly why the man is not interested, and whatever response he provides, it is met with some rationalization as to why he is misinformed, and therefore should change his mind. Playing on a male target's sense of masculinity can also be leveraged in such endeavors: the sadistic question of "why hurt you?" comes to mind here as, in men acknowledging the negative behaviors they have experienced by women, their common response is to ask this question, commonly accompanied with laughter. This not only displays that they are aware of these manipulative behaviors by women, but that they get enjoyment out of the idea that men are negatively affected by them—furthermore displaying a complete lack of compassion, but also a sense of humor paralleling that of psychopaths (see (Im) Plausible Deniability). Additionally, by downplaying the significance of such behavior—generally abuse—through this method, it implies that the "masculine" thing to do is not to learn from this experience, but man up and continue to pursue women, indefinitely. By society's response to men electing to opt out, the problem is not in women viewing their interactions with men as a *Power Struggle wherein any form of manipulation as well as abuse is fair game, which of course naturally sabotages the relationship from the start, but that the man chose wrong.

Handling Argumentative People

A number of scenarios commonly come about wherein engaging with others is not worth it (e.g., narcissistic baiting). For instance, all too often, even if you call someone out on being wrong about something, seemingly, due to the perception of there being an audience, egotism, but also because they may just enjoy arguing, the other party will resort to doubling down, ad hominem attacks, or the use of a red herring wherein a separate argument is presented as to not accept that their original assertion was incorrect. This ego-driven tendency—one that permeates even debates between content creators as they want to be the voice of reason—can be preemptively dealt with as I've come to notice in using a simple technique on multiple occasions. To do this, well, first be sure that you have your facts in order as no one is infallible. Then, prior to even stating your position, inform the other person of the likely modes of reaction they will engage in. Here's an example: you watch one of my videos regarding female nature, post a comment based in reality but it is met with an emotion-based response that is obviously incorrect and/or based in gaslighting. Your response can be something along the lines of, so before I even respond, I already know that you're going to get upset, double down on your initial response, and not listen to a word I'm saying, but...and then you go on to provide your response. It seems that when someone's reaction to others results in emotional escalation, which is commonly coupled with a doubling down on a stance they've invested in, it becomes exceptionally hard to reason with them following this point, and regardless of how rational you are. However, if you bring up this reaction prior to the escalation reaching its maximum intensity (i.e., before you even provide a response/rebuttal), it appears to inhibit the process entirely; perhaps they come to realize that this behavior is predictable, and therefore they do not want to be perceived in that light; but it may also be the case that as they have not escalated to the full extent, they are more likely to be a bit more rational. One particular instance comes to mind wherein I used this technique offline with a woman. She seemingly wanted to engage in doubling down and arguing as indicated by her facial

MANIPULATION 201

expression shifting to one of anger (see The Truth in Anger), hands shaking, and mouth opening only to close shortly after. It appeared that by taking their go-to mode of reaction away, they reached somewhat of a state of paralysis. In this sense, the desire to be unpredictable outweighs the desire to argue, and likely because it means that you would be right again which would be another hit to their ego. Moreover, and unfortunately, if I had *not* used this technique, the woman's desire to argue, and perhaps gaslight, would have outweighed her desire to be right.

The Marketplace IS NOT Your Pet Shop

As F. Roger Devlin put it, "the husband, for his part, feels like the victim of a "bait and switch" sales tactic. One wonders what would become of the human race if women told their boyfriends flat out: "you must marry me so I can stop pretending to love you as you are, and start complaining about all the ways you disappoint me." As is progressively becoming more accepted today as a facet of women's relation to men, they don't necessarily love the *man*, but what he can *do* for her. This also appears to be a part of a superficially agreeable Machiavellian mindset. By not emotionally connecting with the man, paralleling with Dr. David Buss's mate switching hypothesis in that women are always on the lookout for something better, but also the evolutionary explanation that it makes more sense for women in general to not become too attached to any one man due to the dangerous environment and therefore, a high chance of

MANIPULATION 201

loss, Machiavellian women, but I would argue, the average woman, does not emotionally connect with her partner. This form of manipulation is where you may end up with pseudo-compassionate displays in order to garner resources. It would appear that the world has furthermore gotten too safe for women: women use men's negative emotions as a gauge of their commitment during times of conflict which results in the typical male tendency of withdrawing—perhaps during an argument—to negatively impact them. Today, as things tend to be much safer, resulting in there being significantly less conflict than in the past, and therefore, less of a need for relationship conflict, perhaps this tendency to gauge a partner in this manner has become maladaptive. Such a state of affairs appears to result in provocative/sadistic acts by women in order to initiate conflict. In this sense, interestingly, the very metric that women use as a means to gauge a man's investment, and therefore, security, as it is not as forthcoming as a byproduct of the comforts of contemporary society, must be provoked through manipulative acts, and thus, perhaps eliciting the very set of circumstances—i.e., abandonment—that women fear and seek to avoid to begin with. In essence, they are shooting themselves in the foot, but so are men by doing the precariously "masculine" thing: endure the woman's abuse which, as we know, men pass away earlier on average for factors such as heart disease. You know what contributes to heart disease? Stress, which may mean that the better things get, the more women test; and the more women test, the more likely they are to have significantly adverse effects on men's health. How this behavior can play out goes as follows: a man and a woman are dating. To the man, things are going great as there is no drama. His girlfriend, on the other hand, cannot accurately gauge her security within the relationship given that there have been no tests thus far regarding the man's willingness to invest in her outside of, perhaps, the realm of the monetary. This does not sit well with her, resulting in an impending sense of abandonment anxiety. In attempts at assuaging this anxiety, she takes it upon herself to implement some form of testing—a set of circumstances that would have taken place naturally in a more dangerous environment. This testing can take a number of forms and is therefore dependent on the woman's imagination as well as aversion to risk such as bringing up information regarding an ex or perhaps establishing false, or even real, predicaments involving perceived or real danger. Notably, this testing may additionally serve to gauge whether the man can effectively protect her; this especially being the case if the women is low in risk aversion,

MANIPULATION 201

and therefore, more likely to put herself in compromising situations. As for our hypothetical scenario, the woman resorts to bringing up information about an ex which, perhaps makes the man uncomfortable. In this state, the man looks away from his girlfriend, but he misses the vital opportunity to observe that the woman has a rather large smirk on her face. This expression may be indicative of a couple of things:

1. An elicited positive emotional state in that she perceives she has accurately gauged the man's negative emotional state.
2. An elicited positive emotional state in that she has elicited a desired negative emotional response in the man, indicating that he is emotionally attached to her, and therefore relieving her of anxiety.

As an aside, there are women as I've observed—some of which seemingly enjoying eliciting a negative emotional response in people in general—who have engaged in sadistic acts for so long that they have gotten used to attempting to hide the involuntary emotional response. In these cases, they may look away, but the expression is nevertheless apparent to at least some extent. You've likely seen someone attempt to hold in laughter, and this facial expression is similar in that the face unnaturally tends to twitch as the individual is consciously going against the facial manifestation of their true emotional state (see I Can Hardly Contain Myself). The relief women acquire in these situations is only temporary, so although the man may unknowingly serve as a pawn in her sadistic acts, over time, he may decide to abandon her as this recurring behavior results in his skepticism of *her* investment in the relationship as well as unwarranted stress. Perhaps she has proven herself to be of risk to his wellbeing in setting up dangerous predicaments such as being provocative towards outside parties to the relationship wherein he is expected to deal with the consequences of her actions—a scenario requiring that he display his willingness to sacrifice for her. Or, more commonly, she constantly picks fights that are completely unnecessary in the man's eyes. This pursuit of gauging a man's commitment will not invariably be the reason why women engage in such behavior, however. People can end up engaging in the same behavior, but as a consequence of different factors. For instance, you can imagine two people who spend the bulk of their time alone: while one of them could be higher in autism, resulting in them prioritizing things besides people, the other may have faced, perhaps, some form of abuse early on which makes them highly skeptical of people in general. The more recent explosion of Dark Triad traits such as narcissism in women may be playing a role in women's perpetual testing of men and causing unnecessary conflict. As Sam Vaknin recently stated in an interview: "narcissists are very antagonistic. They constantly seek conflict. They introduce aggression into totally unnecessary situations and environments. They're grandiose and they seek attention compulsively." This quote by itself can sum up quite a large number of the accounts of men when it comes to their relationships with women. In considering that these are tendencies of narcissists, a man may end up with a woman engaging in the same provocative/sadistic behaviors as previously mentioned; in this case not with the goal of eliciting a negative emotional response to gauge the man's commitment, but perhaps to elicit a negative emotional response for the sake of eliciting a negative emotional response. It is worth noting, however, that these two reasons for testing are not mutually exclusive: a woman can be heavily narcissistic and test for the commitment of others as is to be expected, but also to garner sadistic supply—perhaps even both at the same time. Of course, in the case of those who are socially informed by conventional "wisdom," they will be inculcated by narratives of women being sugar, spice, and everything nice.

R.P. MENTOR TOKYO

Dr. Cory Clark once said, with regard to women's more recent predominance in academia as well as censoring of certain voices, that "men are relatively more interested in advancing what is empirically correct and women are relatively more interested in advancing what is morally desirable." Similarly, I will say that men are more interested in advancing how women's attraction, and furthermore, psychology, objectively functions and women are relatively more interested in advancing pseudo-altruistic narratives about themselves which they perceive as desirable for establishing a moral image. Narratives that, although bolstering the women are wonderful effect, couldn't be further from the truth and, in fact, when it comes to reality, tend to be completely opposite to how their psychology functions. This has likely played a significant role in the perpetuation of men's false perceptions of women, and especially in times wherein word of mouth was about all men had to go off of. But this, fortunately, is not the case today, and with all the information available, there is an important question I think it would behoove men to ask themselves: what is the basal or instinctive response women have to you? For women, their facial structure elicits a compassionate response, but this is not the case for men, and why it makes sense that you do not see women taking care of them in relationships. Men, on the other hand, but more specifically compassionate men, are more than willing to take care of women in the same manner as they would a household pet as, in both cases, how the pet or woman looks elicits this compassionate response, so they are willing to trade resources for their affection. The man may get joy out of observing the woman's state of happiness when he feeds her as he would a dog getting excited to see him filling its bowl. Women seemingly mimic these visceral compassionate responses men express towards them as a consequence of their neotenous traits, which results in the man projecting. This furthermore makes sense of this reverse beauty and the beast dynamic (see Either You Dominate Me, Or I Dominate You): while the woman mimics the man early on, allowing him to falsely perceive that her psychology functions the way his does, when commitment has been obtained in the form of marriage, she becomes the monster the man is expected to "put in her place." This is in part because she is trying to force the man to fulfil her need for dominance as well as a Dark Triad drama-rich environment. The Marketplace IS NOT Your Pet Shop.

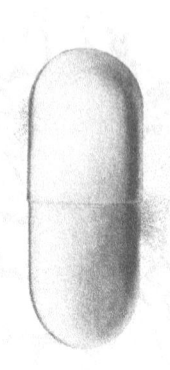

Could You Do Me a Favor?

There are many ways this tactic can play out. One is referred to as weaponized incompetence and you'll commonly see this in the workplace when sharing a space with women. This is when the woman targets the man while viewing her interactions with him as a *Power Struggle and tests the waters by asking for a simple favor. Generally, due in part to women's neotenous traits which elicit a compassionate response in your average man, he is not suspecting anything at all. In her mind, the more she can get the man to do for her, the more she is winning, and perhaps is indicative to her as being desirable as the man does anything she wants. By this reasoning, this may also be perceived as a cue for the man's commitment to her. Again, the man is not viewing the dynamic in this manner at all. Here is a simple example: you're walking with a group of people and a girl behaves in a semi-flirtatious manner towards

MANIPULATION 201

you. She proceeds to ask if you will hold her umbrella for her. Not thinking much of it, you do. After about two minutes of walking while holding it, you give it back to her, and she pretends to forget that you were holding it. A bit later on, she asks if you will hold her drink. She had to use the bathroom, so you go along with it. She comes back out and again pretends to forget that you're holding it. You give the drink back to her. About twenty minutes later she asks you to hold another item and this time you decline. In response she begins to giggle. Women with a past of bullying may also implement this strategy, but in a more aggressive manner wherein, instead of a favor being asked, they will test by *telling* you to do something or perhaps implying that you *should* do something. This can persistently occur every time you run into the manipulator as they are gauging under what circumstances they can make you subservient to them, and once they learn this, they will make a mental note and repeat the process. Similarly in the workplace, women will pretend to be incompetent about tasks that they don't feel like doing or just want to test to see what they can get you to do for them. These perceived wins for them in the *Power Struggle—as you are their real-time strategy-based video game—will likely be used as gossip talking point with other female co-workers as extracting the resources of male attention as well as labor is found desirable as well as indicative of the women's worth. Here too, the man generally is not viewing his interactions with the women present in the same manner. This can be a tough call for men as they may not be able to exactly pinpoint where to draw the line when helping women—when they are genuinely needed, and when they are being taken advantage of which is completely understandable. Women's neotenous traits also aid them in pushing men to think that they should help them as men don't tend to have this problem when interacting with other men. This is also one reason many men have issues with women in the workplace: when work needs to get done, while the men are proactive about it, there are women who resort to attempting to see how much of the work they can delegate to someone else—essentially attempting to play the role of manager regardless of their position. Similarly with marriage, the woman in seemingly most cases becomes a CEO overnight. And when women are tasked, these can also be spaced out so that, especially in a group setting, someone can be asked periodically to take care of a portion of the task so that it goes unnoticed. In these cases, if the man even thinks to go against the woman, he may be left confused as to when providing a favor is warranted or not. This especially being the case when the requests are spaced out. While it becomes rather obvious that the woman is being unreasonable if she asks for 10 things all at the same time, how much the man has done for her may slip under the radar—thus being perceived of as acceptable—if she periodically asks for the same things over time. Again, do note that she *is* keeping tabs on her ability to get the man to do things for her, and she will insist on asking for something if the man is anywhere near her. The problem with this response in men is that it is so ingrained, the man's inclination to aid the women seemingly occurs as some form of autopilot (see Female-Induced Male Paralysis). For the men whose psychology functions in this manner, making an effort to preemptively acknowledge that women *will* engage in manipulative self-serving behaviors prior to meeting them (e.g., on the way to work) will likely prove beneficial. By this framework as well, when interacting with women, ask yourself the following two questions when they ask for a favor:

1. Would I help if this were a man asking for the same favor?
2. Will I resent this person if I do help them?

From here you'll have to go with your gut, but also pay close attention to the woman's face when she asks the favor as she may be smirking or trying to hold it back. Easier said than done for some due to myriad factors such as an upbringing wherein you weren't allowed to set boundaries, but if you can, say no and observe the woman's response. It is a true mark of entitlement when her response is to be upset when doing a "favor" is declined (see The Truth in Anger).

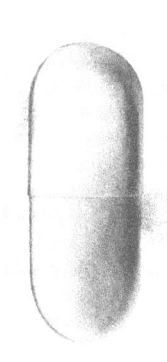

The Parrot Test

This is another manipulation tactic that functions under plausible deniability and is quite easy to overlook. Manipulators are constantly picking up on exploitable cues as well as storing information on their targets. Like a parrot, they may resort to repeating points you brought up in the past as if it were a genuine personal thought. This *is* a test and can be implemented in various scenarios whether it be to make the manipulator appear as a more viable partner, establishing rapport, but also in the act of stealing the ideas of others. In the case of establishing rapport—perhaps by an aspiring *Clinger—this tactic can be implemented in as subtle a manner as repeating a location you visited or movie you really enjoyed at some later time. As for the stealing of ideas, here is an example: you take the time to compile a well thought out take on a particular subject—perhaps in order to create an article for your job.

R.P. MENTOR TOKYO

One of your co-workers which you consider to be a friend, sees the article and agrees that it looks really good. The deadline to submit the article is in about a month. About three weeks later, this "friend" begins speaking with you in a weak tone about a supposed original idea of his that is slightly different than yours but is essentially the same. Notably, during this time, he is looking rather intensely at your face with a bit of discomfort on his and you notice that his hands are slightly shaking (see See No Evil, Hear ~~No~~ Evil). At this point, I would say that it is best for you to turn in your article as soon as possible as this "friend" likely has it in their mind that you won't call them on their behavior and is furthermore leveraging the idea that you are friends to their benefit (see Appeal to Emotion). Of course, you could call them out on their behavior, but you will likely end up receiving an answer based in plausible deniability. People will use your emotions against you. This strategy I have also observed on YouTube: a content producer generates an interesting video that gets a lot of attention. Instead of giving credit, another channel at some point in the future leaves a comment just slightly shifting the idea behind the video as to present it as their own idea, but in all actuality, this shift was not their own either as the newly added information came from another one of the content

MANIPULATION 201

creator's videos that they're stealing from. Again, it is quite easy to overlook this tactic as you may not be suspecting this behavior, nor are the things you said, perhaps, over four months prior, fresh in your mind when the manipulator resorts to repeating it like a parrot.

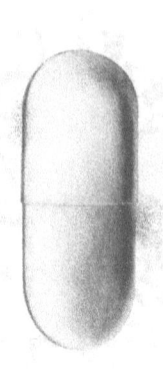

The Machiavellian in Me

Pseudo-compassionate as well as agreeable displays serving to conceal an emotionally detached psychology are the name of the game in Machiavellian land. This plays to women's benefit in, as well as outside of, a relationship context as this mask aids them in garnering a target's resources. Interestingly as well, they may resort to implementing *Appeal to Ego to get the target's defenses down, and in the event these strategies fail, may resort to increasing these behaviors. An example in the workplace would go as follows: your boss is engaging in manipulative acts such as calling you for a sudden meeting right around the time you're supposed to leave the office. Knowing that you have little interest in talking to them to begin with, they will also insist on forcing conversations (see Induced Conversation), but these conversations are presented in a plausibly deniable manner meant to conceal the fact that they

MANIPULATION 201

are aware you don't want to talk to them as they speak in an exaggeratedly kind manner—generally small talk. This is yet another *Power Dynamic wherein they view it as a win when they can force an interaction with you. And if you resort to ignoring them or going against what they want to talk about, this can result in anger (see the Truth in Anger).

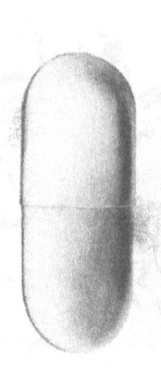

Babe, Meet My Best Friend, Chad!

Interestingly, and in line with women's advantage over men in their ability to get away with cheating, women may attempt to have their long-term partner meet or even befriend their short-term ones. While this state of *affairs* may be framed as just a "friendship" in the eyes of the long-term partner, it serves to establish a triangle of infidelity—perhaps with a sadistic twist. In regular cases, the affair partner is kept secret; however, in the case of this insisted friendship, it provides a plausibly deniable scenario wherein the woman and the "friend" will gaslight the long-term partner into thinking nothing is going on. You can refer to my video on Adina Rivers for what I suspected to be a direct example of this. It is worth noting here that one means by which women select these short-term partners is out of the long-term partner's "friend" group which is the perfect set of circumstances for a *Clinger. There may also exist a sadistic aspect as the woman gets enjoyment out of having the affair partner interacting with the long-term partner. Moreover, if the affair partner, perhaps a *Clinger, views mate poaching as a sport—a trait characteristic of the Dark Triad—or just wants to cause as much damage to their supposed "friend" as possible, they may also garner sadistic supply from such a situation. By establishing such a false friendship, the woman will feel more comfortable in disclosing her interactions with the affair partner, but of course omitting the sexual nature of their interactions. For instance, informing the long-term partner that she plans on meeting or having the affair partner over while he is away. This would furthermore aid the woman in genetically cuckolding the long-term partner while extracting his resources (i.e., a dual-mating strategy). Alternatively, a more overt method of boundary pushing may be prioritized: instead of telling her long-term partner beforehand about meeting with the affair partner, she may just skip this step entirely if she desires to disrespect the man or perhaps aims to elicit sexual jealousy as a means to test his investment in her. An example may go as follows: the woman informs the long-term partner that she let their "mutual male friend" come over, and goes on to ask, don't you remember? I told you before. When in all actuality, this conversation never took place. Such an instance may be accompanied by a smirk whether the woman is aware of it or not. Most likely she is as this tactic is premeditated with the anticipated goal being to elicit an emotional response in order to gauge his investment in her. If a negative emotional response is the outcome of her behavior, she perceives that he is emotionally attached to her to at least some extent. Additionally, one goal, or at least outcome, of women's persistent boundary pushing will be to not only see what she can get away with but wear the man down so that he is less inclined to go against her long-term agenda. One such particular goal of these tireless efforts may be to get the man to tire of checking behaviors perceptibly indicative of cheating as, if accomplished, these behaviors can be engaged in without resistance. That is, of course, if the man does not leave.

Female-Induced Male Paralysis

This is a state that I have not heard anyone bring up yet plays a role in men's susceptibility to particularly women's manipulative behaviors. You can imagine a man in the workplace: a woman insists that he engage in some activity, his body freezes up, and a sense of obligation comes over him regardless of the circumstances. Perhaps it comes down to a consequence of men being raised by single mothers—a state feminists have fought for—and so this dynamic of appeasing the primary authority figure—as to do otherwise as a child equates to death—is extrapolated to other women later in his life. Women are well aware of this state of men feeling obligated, and even in the event their demands fail, they will perpetually attempt to wear men down with demands (see Could You Do Me a Favor?). This starts the cycle of male concessions wherein the woman gets the man to say "yes" to whatever she wants him to do;

yet another example of women viewing their interactions with men as a *Power Struggle. Many men—directly facilitating women's hypoagency—will assert that women don't know that they're engaging in such behavior, but it becomes rather apparent that this is *not* the case if you observe this behavior when other women are around. They resort to watching the woman testing the man, perhaps with a smile, and in anticipation of his response.

I'm Done with the Games

Commonly, women will put behaviors they have either engaged in or manipulation tactics they have been caught off guard by on dating app profiles. In the case of the former, this is an admission of how their psychology functions and can reliably serve as foreshadowing for what you can expect if you were to pair with them. The same goes for those who insist on showcasing traits such as honest: people resort to asserting traits preemptively in the hopes of lowering the guard of others. Similarly, women's dating-app profiles commonly display wording such as "I hate liars." This is yet another preemptive strategy meant to deter manipulators from targeting them but will likely be viewed as a weakness given that it worked before. There may furthermore be a sadistic aspect to this for manipulators given that the last person affected them to such a significant extent that they're still talking about it, so if they get enjoyment out of people's negative emotional responses, this tactic meant to deter this type of person serves as a sort of beacon guiding them straight to them. You may be done with the games, but the games are never done with you.

/noclip

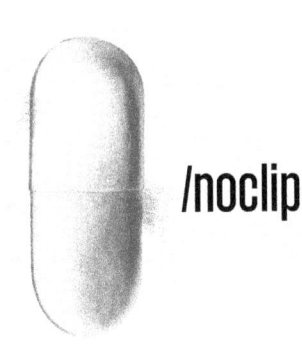

Growing up, I used to play a first-person shooter called Quake. As with many shooters, there is a console wherein you can type commands to alter the game such as making yourself invincible. /noclip was one such command that, when activated, allowed you to glitch completely out of the map and travel through walls to reach any desired destination which was always beneficial for seeing the environment from a new perspective as well as getting around your enemies. In the real world, of course, you can't just magically jump through walls to get around your enemies when need be, but the following two statements will get you pretty close:

1. You may have heard some variant of this before, but many people—seemingly the majority—cannot stand to see you do better than themselves.

2. When you are doing well, many people will, at best, be inclined to load you with their burdens—seemingly to balance things out; and at worst, destroy you.

When you're doing well, this is one time to watch out for the majority of manipulation tactics in this booklet such as that of *Clingers. As they may be highly envious of you, they will try to get in your good graces so as to elevate themselves and would be more than willing to knock you down or replace you in the process. Any vulnerability they perceive can and will be used against you (see The Parrot Test), and this commonly comes in the form of getting you to feel sorry for them while simultaneously exploiting you. For instance, let's say you are making a name for yourself by helping people with a service which has been a huge success. A *Clinger may resort to getting you to feel sorry for their set of circumstances but will then feel entitled to steal ideas or whatever they can from you in a covert manner. Essentially, the goal is to steal your identity and replace you. Thinking back to my old Quake days, it was fun to float around the maps and see what the enemies were doing when they didn't know you were watching them. In the real world, your wellbeing as well as livelihood may be at stake, however, so I hope this information on manipulation amongst the other entries allows you to do the same thing in the real world.

Medical Gynocentrism

Unquestionably, there are some heavily gynocentric aspects to contemporary society. One in particular is the fact that men can end up being forced to pay for another woman's decision to commit paternity fraud. I say decision as women's affair partners in these situations tend to be quite similar to the man they are paired with as a long-term partner. Notably as well, it is known that women tend to have more orgasms with their affair partners which is significant as these pelvic contractions serve to increase the uptake of sperm. Now while many men acknowledge the seeming collusion between women and the courts in exploiting them in this manner, they may not know that Medical Gynocentrism has historically played a significant role in all of this as well. While the highly referenced Dr. Michael Gilding has asserted that high rates of paternity fraud are an "urban myth," it is worth considering results from some studies on paternity discrepancies:

1. A 1989 study finding that, in the case of genetic testing results showing a man is not the father, medical staff at the time would "fail to disclose these results to the social father."
2. One study of medical geneticists in 19 nations finding that 81% would disclose only to the mother, while 15% would claim that either both parents were responsible for the condition, or that the result was anomalous.
3. Another 1989 study finding that of 199 genetic counselors, 93.5% being female, the majority, over 95%, would only inform the mother of misattributed paternity. While the rationalization presented for this was that they were "preserving patient confidentiality and not endangering the family unit/marriage," this points directly to women's in-group bias.
4. Similarly, in 1990, 96% of 677 medical geneticists from 18 countries prioritized protecting the mother's confidentiality over informing the supposed father.
5. In 1994 the Institute of Medicine committee makes the suggestion that misattributed paternity not be volunteered to the father.

6. And in 2014 in the journal Pediatrics, Marissa Palmor and Autumn Fiester "advocate the incorporation of a new clause into the informed consent forms for pediatric genetic testing that clearly states that any incidental information about parentage will not be revealed, regardless of the result."

While similar research should be conducted today to get a better gauge of how likely men are to be informed if they are the father or not following genetic testing, these results do shed light on the fact that there is quite the history of Medical Gynocentrism. Considering how pronounced gynocentrism as well as misandry have become, it shouldn't be to anyone's surprise that a similar mindset has persisted to today.

The Bait and Switch

This mate acquisition tactic is interesting as it sheds light on two things in particular:

1. That women don't realize what men want.
2. That women are more than willing to lie when it comes to pursuing resources.

In surveying women during my time attending university in Japan on whether they would rather pursue a career or become a housewife, it became quite apparent that while they desired to become housewives, they were reluctant to say so. In fact, they would whisper the answer as well as look around to see if anyone was listening, and one older staff member at the university—likely in her mid-to-late 30's—insisted that this desire of hers not be made public. One way women have gone about drawing attention away from this desire is openly asserting that they don't need a man all the while advertising themselves to men in the hopes of landing a provider and making it appear as though it was all his idea as to drive the perceived *Power Struggle in their favor (see also Complain to Maintain). By this method, if the woman is successful, the woman isn't expected to provide much, the man feels as though he is "lucky to have her," and he is less inclined to notice the mate-value discrepancy present. This includes hyper-sexualizing oneself and attending social events as many women hope that they can turn a one-night stand with a high-status man into a long-term relationship. Women will also mimic men in emphasizing their ambitions and goals—real or fabricated—early on in conversations to generate interest, only to drop them later on. As has been admitted by some women, university serves the function of vetting men in order to get an Mrs. degree, and in the event the woman is not successful in landing a partner here—either as she wasn't interested in the men present or prioritized a short-term mating strategy during this time—there is the idea that by prioritizing a career and climbing the corporate ladder, the higher she goes, and regardless of how much she ages, the men around her will pair with her when *she's* ready. There was one fellow at the university who was definitely on his way to success,

MANIPULATION 201

and one of the girls my group and I had interviewed definitely took notice of this as, by the end of the semester, the two were in a relationship. I remember this rather vividly as I was talking to him about something, and once she came around and realized who he was talking to, distinct signs of discomfort, and potentially fear, became apparent in her eyes. Undoubtedly, she remembered our little interview. Now why, oh why, would she have been afraid of me interacting with her then boyfriend? Well, perhaps it was because she didn't want him to know that she wants to become a housewife. Okay, let's say this is correct. Why then, would she not have wanted him to know? Better question: they were already in a relationship, and even if the topic of whether she wanted to work for a living or be a stay-at-home wife never came up, why would she not have wanted him to know? It is likely that when she was attempting to set the foundation for the relationship, she led with her supposed ambitions and goals, and these of course had nothing to do with her actual desires. As one woman put it, "I agree we should be more upfront about our desires. But these days, when women say they want to be housewives, they get called lazy." Women are aware they are engaging in a Bait and Switch, and while what she said is true, it has predominantly been feminists who make such assertions as, if a man is willing to pair with a woman, he tends to expect to play the provider role from the start. In this sense, it is women attempting to hide from the criticisms of other women while being oblivious to, and not attempting to learn, what men desire from them. As lesbian feminists have historically tried to get women away from men, even going as far as to asserting women should form women-only communities and expressing the desire to "destroy the institution of heterosexual sex," this has likely played a role. In all actuality, while women may perceive that they are getting over on men by this Bait and Switch strategy, they may be shooting themselves in the foot as they may have cost themselves relationship opportunities by presenting themselves as career as opposed to family focused.

Something for Nothing

You know the saying: "what's yours is mine, and what's mine is mine." Women are perpetually trying to gain Something for Nothing, and for the most part, this strategy is highly effective. As they possess more neotenous traits which elicit a compassionate response coupled with the framing effect (see The Marketplace IS NOT Your Pet Shop) as well as the implication that there is the chance a giving man can gain sexual access by investing in her, it comes as no surprise that women can easily acquire resources without even investing much effort on their part. Interestingly, there exists an entitled mindset in women which manifests in datamining men to see what they can acquire from them but is expressed in yet another plausibly deniable manner. For instance, a woman may ask you something like what you did over the weekend, what your hobbies are, or more directly, what you're good at. While these kinds of questions generally are meant to establish rapport when conversing with other men, women will raise these questions to gauge what forms of labor they may be able to get out of you (see also Could You Do Me a Favor). As stated, there is a sense of entitlement to this mindset: if you're an honest man who is not prone towards thinking that a simple question serves to provide the woman with some kind of gain, you may explain that, perhaps, you were doing something like building some new shelving or fixing a household appliance. Remember the saying: what's yours is mine, and what's mine is mine. Even upon initially meeting women, they will attempt to extract your labor through this form of datamining. Dr. David Buss has talked about how women want to be able to manipulate their partners to at least some extent and this is one way in which they will check. In fact, this mode of datamining may even serve to tell you if a woman if considering you as a long-term partner. For many men with no interest in dating, however, this testing women engage in just becomes rather annoying and actually has the opposite effect of what the woman was aiming for. While she may have been aiming to make the man closer to her—likely thinking that men inherently enjoy doing things for women; a rather convenient self-serving rationalization—as with engaging in a

MANIPULATION 201

sadistic manner to get a perceived potential partner to express their commitment (see The Marketplace IS NOT Your Pet Shop), the man is actually more likely to abandon her due to finding her personality inherently repulsive. Even when punished by the man cutting contact, however, no lessons are learned which is characteristic of those higher in the Dark Triad and furthermore explains why some women perpetually jump from relationship to relationship engaging in the same behaviors. Insisting that the man provide labor when he is not interested nor pursuing her sexually just comes off as entitled and narcissistic. In many cases, this may not be far from the case: while men have historically had a sexual overperception bias, meaning that they are more prone to think women are sexually interested as it increases their chances of reproductive success, women, I've argued today have switched from a commitment skepticism bias to a commitment overperception bias. As it would have been dangerous for women in the past to avail themselves sexually to men not demonstrating signs of commitment as they may end up pregnant and abandoned, it makes sense that they would be prone towards vetting men to ensure the safety of themselves as well as any ensuing offspring. Today, with the advent of technologies such as the pill and the implementation of factors such as divorce courts, alimony, and child support, we are living in a completely different environment. So much so that many women today purposely pursue becoming a single mother, so a commitment overperception bias appears plausible in my eyes. This is the female equivalent of men's sexual overperception bias in that, the more narcissistic the woman is, the more likely this overperception is to occur. This is how you may end up with women, when initially interacting with men, are already pushing for his labor: she has overperceived the man's commitment from the start by assumption—perhaps blowing out of proportion the significance of the man's body language in an unwarranted ego-inflating manner—resulting in the false perception that the *Power Dynamic is in her favor. The man who is interested in the woman and provides his labor for free is not someone she will respect as a long-term partner, however, as, if they do end up in a relationship—notably, the woman may become bored of him prior to this point—she essentially becomes a CEO overnight with a more than willing male subordinate.

The Fun Police of Stockholm

Stockholm Syndrome results in victims of abuse growing attached to their abuser(s). Experts on this syndrome emphasize four conditions for its development:

1. The captor treats their victims humanely.
2. The captives and captors have significant face to face interaction which provides opportunities to bond with one another.
3. The captives feel that law enforcement personnel are not doing their jobs well enough.
4. The captive thinks that the police and other authorities do not have their interest at heart.

While this syndrome is more so acknowledged in situations with hostages, women can also induce this condition in men perhaps inadvertently through means such as circumcision, but we will use the following example to make sense of how: a man is met with aggression via text or in person *when*, around the time *of*, and/or even *after* the time that he planned to go out—perhaps with his friends. This abuse (e.g., abruptly becoming disagreeable or argumentative) serves as an insidious strategy to train the man to associate being away with punishment. This would further serve to establish dependency *on her*, and therefore, commitment as well as the maintaining of resources. The perpetrator may not even be cognizant of this trend: perhaps a state of discontentment is elicited when the partner is away as a ramification of some form of abandonment anxiety. In other cases, however, these acts may be malicious—both situations having the same effect on the target with the former of which, likely coming off as more plausible given that she genuinely perceives her thoughts as well as behaviors to be legitimate, and therefore, justified. Plausible deniability in relation to these abruptly-surfacing arguments notwithstanding, that the abuser treats the man humanely at other times—as is naturally the case in relationships—bonding occurs with the relationship not being questioned, causing these acts to slip completely under the radar. Moreover, the women's neotenous traits in eliciting a compassionate response, would further aid in this bonding process as well as the perception that she cannot play the role of manipulative aggressor (hypoagency). Whether implemented maliciously or otherwise, this coercive act regresses the man, or chips away at him, until he is but a mere shell of his former self—a child, vulnerable and dependent, and worn down to a state of not wanting to displease his mother. This is an extrapolation of the mother-son dyad playing out on an unconscious level which explains the man's elicited fear as well as reluctance to leave: it's not that the man is afraid of enduring physical blows by the abuser, but that as was the case in childhood, protection was in the hands of the mother, and thus, she was perceived of as being in complete control as to go against her would mean death. Such a trauma bond is rather hard to break and from an outside eye looking in, the connection makes no sense which, in line with the fourth condition for developing Stockholm syndrome, friends and family members of the abused who suggest ending the relationship are viewed as the enemy instead of people trying to help. To form one of these bonds, intermittent—on and off—positive as well as negative behavior, bonding, high arousal periods, and a power differential are required—all facets of the aforementioned relationship scenario. The woman is also adept at gauging the man—as is the case with those higher in the Dark Triad (see Soul Gazer)—bringing about a power differential; she intermittently engages in argumentation as to gain control in a malicious or unconscious manner; and as naturally occurs in a relationship, high arousal in the form of sexual contact as well as bonding occurs. Additionally, in purposely provoking arguments, this not only keeps the target's focus on the partner while they're away—a clear desire of a narcissistic individual, but also someone desperate to ensure security—as well as trains them over time to associate time away as punishment, but likely ultimately instills a self-perpetuating sense of isolation as being with the partner is one of the few times the target isn't punished, or at least, is punished less (i.e., their newfound comfort zone). The woman makes the man feel as though he is in the wrong, there is a make-up period, and then the cycle repeats. In considering that men tend to withdraw from fights within relationships and given that they may be perceived of as occurring at random, this causes the man to walk on eggshells. Such a set of circumstances may cause anxiety, depression, safety and comfort seeking as well as a subordinate self-perception.

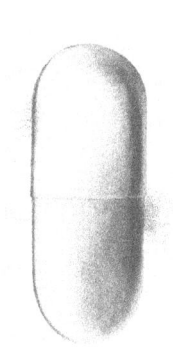

Soul Gazer

While there is a segment in this book titled *The Golden Rule, I could refer to this one as the golden realization. Manipulators have been endowed with the rather useful ability to observe and gauge those around them for factors such as weak points which they can use to exploit them. One such method can be rather interesting but perhaps off-putting to observe. This is a blank—although sometimes accompanied with a smirk—stare tending to, although not invariable, be preceded by, used with, or even following statements/questions, and serving the purpose of gauging your responses including, but not limited to words, facial expressions, body language, and movements. Interestingly, the speech pattern accompanied by this trancelike state of the manipulator, from what I've observed, is rather predictable: paralleling the research findings on unreliable and deceptive speech in *See No

Evil, Hear ~~No~~ Evil, you will notice that the person speaks slowly which is indicative of more cognitive effort being used—perhaps juggling their words as well as manipulative tendencies, and sticks out as at no other point in the conversation did they sound like this. Not only this, but their voice comes off as rather weak and tends to trail off with perhaps a rising intonation at the end. Again, honesty has been associated with falling intonation meaning the pitch becomes lower towards the *end* of a word/statement as well as the voice being louder from the beginning. This is the exact opposite vocal signature of manipulators when they are using the skill of Soul Gazer.

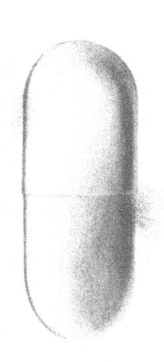

The Substance of Life

Although not necessarily about a manipulation tactic—if anything, it's how you manipulate yourself—it is something important I've come to realize over the years: the use of substances (e.g., alcohol in my case, but perhaps drugs) can have a significant effect on your life, and in more ways than one. As for myself, not only was I drinking heavily from age 17-26, but it seemed to shift my psychology to unlocking more Dark Triad traits throughout those years—even when I was sober as there appeared to be some kind of residual or spillover effect. This reversed, resulting in some form of mental reboot following my quitting alcohol, but what I did learn was that like attracts like. By this I mean that throughout those years, the people that I chose to be around—predominantly for the purposes of going out and drinking more—were also higher in the Dark Triad which I do not think was by chance.

R.P. MENTOR TOKYO

This all hit me the longer I stayed sober as their manipulative tendencies as well as facial expressions indicative of sadism such as smirking began to stick out to me; something I never noticed when I was drinking alcohol with them. In retrospect, and following my researching this subject, it doesn't come as a surprise as substance abuse along with promiscuity *are* associated with psychopathy. Now understandably, people enjoy the feeling of being intoxicated—myself included—but it is to your benefit to quit as it may put you in a clearer mental state to see who you should discard for a better life. The same goes for any other substance that puts you in an altered state. At this point, I've actually dropped many people from my hometown as well as those I've met during my time in Japan, and at the time of my writing this, am considering moving to another country.

I Need to Get Back at Them

The desire to get back at those who have wronged you, and especially when you can't perceive that you've done anything to deserve it, is a normal response to having been abused by others. It is worth coming to the realization, however, that such a mindset plays to the manipulator's benefit as they crave a drama-rich environment—again, a trait characteristic of those higher in the Dark Triad, and an unmistakably common trait in women today. The more they prod you to get a negative emotional response, the more likely you are to provide them this through retaliation which is exactly what they want. Perhaps you are in a relationship with a sadistic partner who constantly prods you. By retaliating, they would surely use this one reaction to justify however much abuse they targeted you with in order to make it appear as though they are the victim. Thinking I Need to Get Back at Them stems from not only being wronged, but as is the case with female manipulators, there is the added layer of the assertion that disengaging is not "masculine" which is yet another case of *Precarious Masculinity meant to make you further serve as a source of masochistic/sadistic supply. By planting this seed in your mind, you are not only more likely to keep engaging to set a perceived wrong right, but you may also find yourself thinking that you're being weak for not doing so which is what the manipulator wants. A game of *Monkey in the Middle in a workplace comes to mind here. These people need this back-and-forth dynamic, so if you can, your best option is to leave. This being regardless of what they, or anyone else says such as being able to endure their abuse builds character, is masculine, or whatever other rationalization they put forward pushing you to continue in this *Power Struggle as a source of someone else's narcissistic supply. Your cognitive energy is much better used elsewhere.

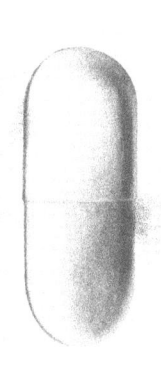

So, What Can You Do?

In reading this book, I sincerely hope that it aids you in not only pinpointing manipulators from your past—perhaps still clinging to you—but also the many manipulation tactics that will surely be used against you in the future. Again, I'll state that by exposing what you're learning to others—and I use the word learning as you'll want to reread this book multiple times as well as reference it when people's actions seem off—it can make you a target if the other party is a manipulator, so be careful about who you share this information with. It may very well be best to remain aware while maintaining an air of obliviousness. Back when I had an interest in studying Japanese, I had it in my mind that I would learn the language, but not let people know. The reason for this was that many Japanese people assume that non-Japanese people don't speak the language, so they would commonly feel rather comfortable speaking badly about these people within earshot of them. Similarly, by internalizing the manipulation tactics laid out in the preceding pages while not making those around you aware of your newfound knowledge, they will feel comfortable using them—sometimes in a more careless manner as they assume you're oblivious—to test to see what they can get away with. And when this occurs, you'll have the upper hand as you have been equipped to know what to expect, and whether you should discard them or not. It's like being able to use the */noclip command, but in real life. It is unfortunate, however, that the world has become so dysfunctional; and if you're not someone who enjoys *Power Dynamics, with the number of Dark Triad people running around, you'll have no choice but to deal with them in any environment wherein you're made to interact with people on an ongoing basis such as in the workplace. This especially being the case if you're working with women as they inherently view their interactions with men through a power-dynamic lens. From their perspective, it's *Either You Dominate Me, Or I Dominate You which is a form of sexual harassment as she is forcing a dominant response in the same manner as a man may insist on pursuing a particular woman for a date in the same setting. Either way she's enjoying your reactions as, in the case of the former, she gains arousal by gaining access to dominance; and as for the latter, sadistic supply as she has become the dominator. What she won't do, however, is just let you do your job as there exists a parallel between narcissists and women: narcissists, like women, feed off of the emotional responses of others. And children, like narcissists, and furthermore like women, would rather have positive *or* negative emotional responses as opposed to indifference. And as many are quite sadistic as well as higher in the Dark Triad, it appears that they aim for the latter. In this sense, it is likely better for many men today to work remote. Do note, however, that like attracts like, so in the event you have to take on an in-person role, if the interviewer at a company displays signs of Dark Triad traits such as narcissism, they will likely hire similar people—perhaps resulting in you not getting the job if you don't harbor or express the same traits during the interview process. If you do, however, do realize that your coworkers may harbor these traits as well. All things considered, it likely goes without saying that living alone will also be to your benefit. Good luck out there.

References

Buss, D. M. (2016). *The evolution of desire: Strategies of human mating.* Basic Books.

Cantor, C., & Price, J. (2007). Traumatic entrapment, appeasement and complex post-traumatic stress disorder: Evolutionary perspectives of hostage reactions, domestic abuse and the Stockholm syndrome. Australian & New Zealand Journal of Psychiatry, 41(5), 377–384. https://doi.org/10.1080/00048670701261178

Cohen, S., Schulz, M. S., Weiss, E., & Waldinger, R. J. (2012). Eye of the beholder: The individual and dyadic contributions of empathic accuracy and perceived empathic effort to relationship satisfaction. Journal of Family Psychology, 26(2), 236–245. https://doi.org/10.1037/a0027488

Devlin, F. R. (2020). Sexual utopia in power: The Feminist Revolt Against Civilization. Ministry of Love.

Drahota, A., Costall, A., & Reddy, V. (2008). The vocal communication of different kinds of smile. *Speech Communication*, *50*(4), 278–287. https://doi.org/10.1016/j.specom.2007.10.001

Goupil, L., Ponsot, E., Richardson, D., Reyes, G., & Aucouturier, J.-J. (2021). Listeners' perceptions of the certainty and honesty of a speaker are associated with a common prosodic signature. *Nature Communications*, *12*(1). https://doi.org/10.1038/s41467-020-20649-4

Gunderson, C. A., Vo, T. V., Harriot, B., Kam, C., & ten Brinke, L. (2022). In search of duping delight. Affective Science, 3(3), 519–527. https://doi.org/10.1007/s42761-022-00126-5

Hercher, L., & Jamal, L. (2016). An old problem in a new age: Revisiting the clinical dilemma of misattributed paternity. *Applied & Translational Genomics*, *8*, 36–39. https://doi.org/10.1016/j.atg.2016.01.004

Kenrick, D. T., Neuberg, S. L., Zierk, K. L., & Krones, J. M. (1994). Evolution and Social Cognition: Contrast Effects as a Function of Sex, Dominance, and Physical Attractiveness. Personality and Social Psychology Bulletin, 20(2), 210–217. https://doi.org/10.1177/0146167294202008

Logan, M. H. (2018). Stockholm Syndrome: Held hostage by the one you love. Violence and Gender, 5(2), 67–69. https://doi.org/10.1089/vio.2017.0076

Lucassen, A., & Parker, M. (2001). Revealing false paternity: Some ethical considerations. The Lancet, 357(9261), 1033–1035. https://doi.org/10.1016/s0140-6736(00)04240-9

Meston, C. M., & Buss, D. M. (2010). *Why women have sex: Women reveal the truth about Thier sex lives, from adventure to revenge (and everything in between)*. St. Martin's Griffin.

Oyeyemi, Abayomi & Onigbinde, Oluwanisola & Lateef, Idowu & Onyemah, Teresa & Eni-Olorunda, Tolu & Correspondence, Abayomi & Ajagbe, Abayomi & Oluwanisola, Ajagbe & Onigbinde, Akanji. (2023). Stockholm syndrome: Causes, implications, and way out. 1-05.

"Psychology in pathology: Stockholm syndrome", International Journal of Emerging Technologies and Innovative Research (www.jetir.org | UGC and issn Approved), ISSN:2349-5162, Vol.9, Issue 4, page no. ppb229-b235, April-2022, Available at : http://www.jetir.org/papers/JETIR2204130.pdf

Pencarinha, D. F., Bell, N. K., Edwards, J. G., & Best, R. G. (1992). Ethical issues in Genetic Counseling: A comparison of M.S. Counselor and medical geneticist perspectives. Journal of Genetic Counseling, 1(1), 19–30. https://doi.org/10.1007/bf00960081

Reynolds, T., Howard, C., Sjåstad, H., Zhu, L., Okimoto, T. G., Baumeister, R. F., Aquino, K., & Kim, J. H. (2020). Man up and take it: Gender bias in moral typecasting. Organizational Behavior and Human Decision Processes, 161, 120–141. https://doi.org/10.1016/j.obhdp.2020.05.002

Schmitt, D. P., & Buss, D. M. (2018). Sex differences in short-term mating preferences. *Encyclopedia of Evolutionary Psychological Science*, 1–7. https://doi.org/10.1007/978-3-319-16999-6_3721-1

Thompson, D. (1992). Against the dividing of women: Lesbian feminism and heterosexuality. Feminism & Psychology, 2(3), 387–398. https://doi.org/10.1177/0959353592023006

Vaknin, S., & Rangelovska, L. (2015). Malignant self-love: Narcissism revisited: Narcissists, psychopaths, and abusive relationship. Narcissus Publications.

Weeden, J., & Kurzban, R. (2016). The hidden agenda of the political mind: How self-interest shapes our opinions and why we won't admit it. Princeton University Press.

Wertz, D. C., & Fletcher, J. C. (1989). Ethical problems in prenatal diagnosis: A cross-cultural survey of medical geneticists in 18 nations. Prenatal Diagnosis, 9(3), 145–157. https://doi.org/10.1002/pd.1970090302

Whitchurch, E. R., Wilson, T. D., & Gilbert, D. T. (2010). "He loves me, he loves me not . . . ": Uncertainty Can Increase Romantic Attraction. Psychological Science, 22(2), 172–175. https://doi.org/10.1177/0956797610393745

https://www.psychologytoday.com/intl/blog/machiavellians-gulling-the-rubes/201610/briffaults-law-women-rule

https://www.youtube.com/watch?v=MrcjJafRfNg

Milton Keynes UK
Ingram Content Group UK Ltd.
UKHW022223050424
440549UK00004B/185

9 798224 174980